UNDERSTANDING
Dressage Training

Angela Niemeyer Eastwood with Andrea Hessay

THE CROWOOD PRESS

First published in 2011 by
The Crowood Press Ltd
Ramsbury, Marlborough
Wiltshire SN8 2HR

www.crowood.com

British Library Cataloguing-in-Publication Data
A catalogue record for this book is available from the British Library.

ISBN 978 1 84797 233 0

Disclaimer
The Authors and Publishers shall have neither liability nor responsibility
to any person or entity with respect to any loss or damage caused or
alleged to be caused directly or indirectly by the information contained
in this book. While the book is as accurate as the Authors can make it,
there may be errors, omissions and inaccuracies.

Typeset by Jean Cussons Typesetting, Diss, Norfolk
Printed and bound in Singapore by Craft Print International Ltd

Contents

Dedication

To our families: Thomas and Natasha, Angela's children (both riders in their own right), for the joy they bring her. Also Gaye, Andrea's sister, who has heard more about horses and dressage over the years than anyone should have to listen to, despite her own almost total lack of interest in matters equestrian! And to Hemmingway: the Grand Prix horse who nearly was! (He died of an aneurism two months before his GP debut – his picture is on the back cover and on page 171.)

Acknowledgements

Grateful thanks are due to Christoph Hess for the foreword; to Inger Bryant for giving us so much of her valuable time and knowledge to read through, amend and correct – always patient and always positive; to Kate Attlee and Corbière II (Charlie), the nine-year-old Hessen gelding owned by Ann Willetts – we are most grateful to Ann, Kate and Charlie; also to Rob Renirie, Jo Beavis, Liz Launder and Russell Guire for their valuable contributions; and to Kevin Sparrow for his inspirational photographs – thanks also to the riders, horses and owners who appear in his photographs. Additional photography is by Sjoert Pegge (Netherlands), Fotohaus Kiepker (Germany) and Andrea Hessay, and we are grateful to Dianne Breeze for her precise drawings and diagrams.

Acknowledgement is due to the memory of Nick Williams, a charming and learned man not afraid to have opinions and voice them convincingly; also to the many authors of books on all aspects of equestrianism; to the teachers, trainers and pupils all over the world whom we have known, worked with, watched, listened to, learned from, and tried to emulate; and finally to the many horses we have been privileged to know and love over a combined total of 100 years, and counting!

We have used many sayings and have credited their creators if known. 'Unknown' next to a saying means that we have not been able to find out from where, and from whom, it originally came.

OPPOSITE: *Angela Niemeyer Eastwood; Kate Attlee on Corbière II (Cockpit x Lousiana) and Ann Willetts.*

Nadonna. (Courtesy of Mrs K. Sparrow)

Foreword

Twenty years ago biomechanics, core stability, gait analysis and sports science were not terms in everyday use in sport, and certainly not in equestrian sport. The horse world has been catching up ever since, and now, in 2010, these aids to equestrianism are centre stage.

Through highly technical computer and camera analyses, we have advanced our understanding of the way in which a horse moves, and how we can use this knowledge to ride and train him in a way that maximizes his potential and minimizes any damage. Through similar analyses we also understand better how we must keep our bodies in balance to use them to the best effect on our horses.

People such as veterinarian and rider Dr Gerd Heuschmann; veterinarian and research scientist Dr Hilary Clayton; equine and human physical therapist Dr Narelle Stubbs; farrier Rob Reniries; Professor Eckart Meyners; and others too numerous to name, have pioneered a better way forwards to ensure horses' wellbeing.

It isn't enough any more just to aim to ride correctly. Thoughtful riders use the research and knowledge available to help themselves and their horses to perform to their best levels – the demands and expectations of the sport of dressage have risen exponentially in recent years, and the welfare of the horse should be at the forefront of every rider's mind. Coaches/trainers have moved on from merely instructing to a more holistic approach that encourages their pupils to take responsibility for their learning and their horses' training.

Modern sport horses are bred for performance, with more and more of them capable of producing stunning athleticism in their paces. However, such paces place big demands on their physique and the ability of their riders, and riders should use the advances in preventative and treatment therapies and veterinary care to do the best they can for continued health and success.

This book explains dressage training, as its title makes clear, but it also encourages horse owners, riders and trainers to look beyond what is written and to search out the optimal ways forward for their partners – their horses.

Christoph Hess
Deutsche Reiterliche Vereinigung e.V. (FN)
Bundesverband für Pferdesport und Pferdezucht

Christoph Hess is the Director of Training and Education at the FN (German Equestrian Federation) in Warendorf, Germany; he is a world-renowned and respected international judge and trainer.

Preface

Dressage is a long-held passion for us both, and this book was born out of a desire to share the information and knowledge acquired over many years of involvement with horses and training. In the end, horses are the teachers and, if you let them, they teach subjects way beyond what might be imagined. A life with horses is never dull, and each day brings fresh challenges, joys and heartaches. It's a certainty that there is no such thing as a perfect horse, but the search for 'the one' goes on. This horse of a lifetime may not be a top competition horse, but he or she will be the one that remains in the memory long after life has faded.

Dressage training hasn't changed greatly over the centuries, and the principles laid down by the Riding Masters are as pertinent now as they have ever been. Where changes have come, they are mostly in the sports science sector – for horses and riders – and a more holistic sport has emerged.

However, in the twenty-first century, instant gratification has infiltrated the horse world, to the extent that there is sometimes less emphasis on doing things properly and progressively, and more emphasis on success in the public domain by whatever means.

There are some outstanding riders and trainers, there are some outstanding, stunning and amazing equine athletes, and sometimes the two species come together – at that point, dressage is the art it's cracked up to be: and there's nothing better, in our totally unbiased opinions!

We have tried to explain our understanding of dressage training as clearly as we can, with the goal in mind of enthusing riders to attain the best standards. Very often, if you do something for the sheer love of it, success follows – whatever success means to you.

Angela Niemeyer Eastwood and Andrea Hessay

1 Introduction

There's something about the outside of a horse that's good for the inside of a man.

(Winston Churchill)

THOUGHTS ON TRAINING

This is a book about dressage and the nitty gritty of training. Thus it's also about humility and the grace to accept that, more often than not, it's not the horse who didn't understand, but the human who didn't explain well enough.

Training horses has taken up most of our lives so far and is our passion; we hope to enthuse and inform you within these pages so that you can find a similar pleasure. Although we've written about how training should be, we acknowledge here that it's not always that simple in the real world – but that doesn't alter the basic principles.

We're very grateful to have been given this opportunity to expound the knowledge and experience gained over many years. Perhaps there's a certain arrogance in assuming that you know enough to write a book, and perhaps this is true if you think you know better than everyone else. We prefer to think of it as sharing knowledge whilst stimulating discussion and dialogue. We don't want to reinvent the wheel, but there are a lot of people out there who aren't sure what the wheel is or what it's for, so we hope this book will make the function of the wheel a little clearer!

We've used a great many photographs, which we hope you will study to find the qualities we thought worthy of your attention; in most of them it's possible to find some fault either with the rider or the horse – but isn't that really the point? You will find that we have used the same photograph in different chapters to illustrate various points. You will also find that there are a couple of photographs of riders not wearing hats – their choice, and we choose not to judge.

There's no such creature as a perfect horse or rider – thank goodness, because the imperfections are the reasons that the playing fields of dressage remain relatively level!

The 'Look of Eagles' – proud, aloof, self-confident, calm.

We think that our subject is relevant to everyone who would like to communicate with, and be in control of, their horse, thus allowing a wonderful partnership to be developed to the full. Elsewhere riding has been defined as 'the art of keeping a horse between you and the ground'. This is a lot less silly than it might sound – after all, you certainly can't ride if you don't have access to a horse on which to do it.

Racing drivers, footballers, opera singers, actors, painters, swimmers and so on usually learn their 'trade' to a high level before they expect to be good – but this is not necessarily the case with riders! 'Do it and be damned' is fine if you have only yourself to consider – but we always have a horse to think about as well. Nor is it a wildly successful approach to assume that riding is something one absorbs as one goes along, and that the horse should know what to do and how to do it.

The many books we have read never seemed, to us, to give all the information or consider all the angles we thought they should. But one day into starting this book, we discovered why! The explanations become endless, trying to cover every eventuality, and the end product could be even lengthier and more complex than this attempt...

So as a nod towards brevity we've left out many possible chapter headings, including conformation, paces (gaits), horse purchase, stable management, fitness and feeding regimes, breaking in, young horse production, detailed descriptions of Grand Prix training and movements including piaffe and passage, show jumping and cross-country, all of which can be read about in detail elsewhere. In the Bibliography you will find the details of several good, informative books that we have dipped into as part of our research, quite a few of which discuss in depth the subjects that we haven't covered.

For word economy and simplicity, we've used the masculine form throughout – apologies to any feminists, human or equine! For further simplification, we have explained all the exercises in the various chapters as being done on the left rein, that is, with the horse going round to the left in whatever field, outdoor school or indoor arena you do your training. Please note that, irrespective of whether you are riding on the left or right rein in a school situation, 'inside' or 'outside' denotes the direction of flexion or bend on that rein.

We've also used the word 'wall', which we've taken in a very broad sense to mean the outside track of an arena, whether fenced, walled, delineated by the edge of the track, or a hedge at the edge of a field. We know it really means an indoor school wall, and we also know that a great many of you don't have access to an indoor school; but we wanted to use one term as a cover-all, otherwise the word count of this book would have been even longer than it is.

It doesn't matter if the person who helps you with the training of both you and your horse is called an instructor, a teacher, a trainer or a coach (we've used the word 'trainer' throughout). What does matter is that you can work together, and that you make progress in your desired direction.

THE BEDROCK OF TRAINING

We have concentrated on the basic training that would benefit any horse, whatever the discipline for which he is intended, but particularly dressage. To say that we repeat ourselves during the course of this book is a massive understatement – 'the basics' are the bedrock of anything you want to do in training, so it's impossible to repeat yourself too often! You will soon discover that 'balance' is one of the most frequently used words in this book. It is at the root of everything you and your horse do together.

Gustav Steinbrecht (1808–85) said, 'Ride your horse forwards and keep him straight.' General

Alexis l'Hotte (1825–1904) added *'calmly'* to this, and these principles hold just as true today as when these two learned trainers coined the expressions. 'Ride your horse calmly forwards and keep him straight.'

How people learn varies from person to person, or perhaps more accurately, from personality to personality. Thus training is an ongoing and constantly evolving process, which needs to take account of many factors: what a person does for a living can give an indication of how they function and the way they learn; what ambitions they have for themselves and their horse; what their physical limitations might be (this is not always apparent from a mere visual inspection) and what sort of horse

they have; how confident they are; and how they see the role of the rider/trainer.

'SWOT' stands for 'strengths', 'weaknesses', 'opportunities', 'threats'. 'Strengths' are your own helpful attributes; 'weaknesses' are your own unhelpful or harmful attributes; 'opportunities' are external conditions that might be helpful; 'threats' are external conditions that might be unhelpful or harmful. This (self-) analytical technique can be an invaluable tool to use to give both trainer and pupil an insight into the qualities that can be brought out in training, and the areas that might need development or adjustment to maximize the training. (Google SWOT for further information.)

We are quite clear that training involves, first and foremost, the rider. If you haven't got an independent, centred, balanced riding position at all paces (and that includes sitting to the trot!), then at best you're a passenger, and at worst a liability to both yourself and your horse. No one is perfect, and a work in progress is the way forwards. In sports psychology, four states of competence are recognized: unconscious incompetence; conscious incompetence; conscious competence; and unconscious competence (being on 'automatic'). The first state can feel quite all right – blissful ignorance being another way to describe it! The fourth state is, of course, the most desirable and the one we should all work towards.

The rider we have in mind is someone who fits in riding with a job and/or family commitments – which covers most of us. The concepts and practicalities that people struggle with are those we have tried to address in these pages because they apply to the many riders capable of great improvement, if only their understanding could be translated into action. Probably the most difficult scenario is a novice rider who buys an inexperienced horse of whatever age. There are fields and training yards full of horses that prove this simply doesn't work,

SCHOOLMASTER HORSES

There are schoolmaster horses out there which, with the help of a good trainer seen regularly, can 'teach' the novice rider the necessary feel before he takes on a less experienced horse.

A word here about schoolmaster horses: these are invaluable if well trained to a high enough level (at least medium, and preferably advanced medium or above) as long as the person who buys and rides one understands that it is up to the rider to learn to ride the horse – only then will the 'buttons' that people assume advanced horses possess (and they do!) become activated. Such horses will not, *per se*, 'teach' someone to become an advanced rider! (This might sound self-evident, but experience suggests otherwise.) Furthermore an advanced horse doesn't stay at that level unless he is frequently 'topped up' by an experienced rider, who reminds him of what he knows and generally keeps him 'up to par'.

and 'We'll learn together' is a phrase that strikes despair into the heart of the most optimistic trainer. It can be done, of course, but it is a project that needs daily supervision, immense dedication, tenacity, and not a little bravery, time and money.

A great many of us ride alone or with a friend, with lessons quite spaced out, so it's easy to get into habits and ways of riding that don't always produce the results you thought they would. Arena mirrors help, and being regularly filmed is also useful to keep a check on yourself.

● Everything you do on top of your horse, and how you do it, is 'training', or at least habit forming, so doing it the best way you can makes sense. The horse can't differentiate between those aids you meant to give and those you have given inadvertently, nor does he know what's acceptable and what isn't unless you make it plain and reward the good!

It's a bit like riding a bicycle – if you sit straight and hold the handlebars evenly and pedal, it's not too difficult to get your bike to go where you want it to without it weaving all over the road. If you lean to one side, then the bike heads that way whatever you do with the handlebars. If your balance is suspect and you wobble about, then the bike wobbles with you. If you stop pedalling, the bike will eventually stop through lack of power, or if you happen to be going downhill at the time, it will run away with you because you are not controlling the speed.

Clearly, you need to be in control of your own body and balance. And when you've learned to sit correctly, it's good to gain the experience of riding as many horses as you can so that you have a depth of knowledge from which to turn yourself into a trainer of horses – even if this means, for you, training your once-in-a-lifetime horse.

Having a Goal

Success: what this is varies according to whom you speak. We all have different, and valid, goals that are very much our own business – but it is vital that you do have a goal. That way you'll progress in skill, understanding and safety. Riding is a potentially dangerous sport at any level, and the better trained your horse, the safer you're both likely to be. Dreams are different from goals – important, perhaps, but try to be sufficiently pragmatic to set achievable goals that are more likely to set you on the road to success.

When riding and training, challenge yourself and your horse regularly and come out of your joint comfort zones. Kyra Kyrklund talks about three zones: comfort, stretch and panic. If both rider and horse are in the first zone, nothing much happens and not much progress is possible; in the second zone, it's handy if the rider is comfortable and relaxed so the horse picks that up and stays settled and calm when learning new things; the horse's panic zone can be approached as long as the rider is in one of the first two zones. Where you definitely don't want to be is in the panic zone at the same time as each other, because it is not a zone where anything good is learned or happens.

Finding the right balance so training can progress smoothly and calmly is something that takes time and experience; therefore don't be afraid to make mistakes, but turn them into learning opportunities. Kyra is famous for using the saying, 'If you always do what you've always done, you'll always get what you always got'.

Then there's the horse. Just as it's true that some of us are more athletically built and better put together than others, so it's true of horses. Jumping horses come in all shapes and sizes, and some unlikely looking horses are amazing jumpers. Dressage horses, or at least horses whose owners want to ride dressage, also come in all shapes and sizes – some with bodies much more conducive to their ability to perform the movements than others that are more physically challenged. This doesn't matter too much if the rider accepts these limitations, but where it becomes an issue is when a horse is physically unable to carry out what is required of him. Conformation really does matter, but – and it's a big 'but' – it's extraordinary how athletic ability and trainability can make up for all sorts of conformational shortcomings. Actually, this probably applies just as much to people as to horses!

Dressage tests are about showing off the quality of the horse's training and the quality of the paces within that training. There is no value in movements done incorrectly, under tension, or without quality. Rather, it should be a demonstration of the harmonious partnership between horse and rider, the ease with which movements are performed, and the pleasure of riding a supple, cooperative horse. The value of testing yourself and your horse in competition is to get an outsider's more objective view of your progress (and, let's be honest, to increase the value of the horse; to qualify for championships; and for the perceived kudos – always supposing that you do well, of course!).

Getting Started

Before you wonder if we're ever going to get started, something more. We've had to make some assumptions in order to start, and these are (in no particular order) that:

- you have a horse to ride
- your horse is properly broken in and that you can stay on
- he understands voice commands
- you can lunge your horse, on both reins, at all paces
- your tack fits him, and you, correctly and comfortably
- you have an independent seat at all paces (or you're working on it!)

- you've done enough reading and/or watched enough DVDs, and had enough lessons, to have some basic knowledge
- you have help with ongoing training
- you have somewhere to ride
- your horse is physically able to do what you want (old enough, fit, sound), and mentally capable (not homicidal, suicidal or just plain crazy).

Kyra Kyrklund calls the acquisition, or perhaps the retention, of knowledge her 'toolbox' and this is certainly one of our aims with this book – to give you as much of our acquired knowledge, or as many 'tools', as we can.

One thing: your horse is *not* a tool. If you treat him as such, you're not likely to be rewarded by the harmonious partnership possible, and desirable, between two living beings.

As with most things, it pays to be flexible and open-minded as what worked last week may neither work nor be appropriate next week – and, with experience, you will find that this is quite normal. Something that works with 80 per cent of horses won't work with the other 20 per cent, and vice versa, and sometimes it might be necessary to find a somewhat circuitous route to achieve your goals.

And that's when a toolbox with plenty of tools in it is particularly valuable.

THE HORSE

Let's look at things from the horse's viewpoint.

Born wild, with all natural fright and flight instincts fully intact, the young horse is able to walk, trot, canter, buck and kick from a few hours old, and constitutionally is not built for anything but roaming and eating. But just when life is looking interesting, there's a plentiful supply of food, you've got friends to play with and Mum to run to when things get worrying, 'they' come along and take you away from

How it is naturally!

everything you know. You're put in a small 'prison', and your mum is nowhere to be seen; if you're lucky, you'll be turned out again with your friends for long enough to grow into a young horse of two or three years old.

Meanwhile, 'things' are put on you and you're led about, often to places you don't want to go; your teeth and feet are rasped and banged; you're put into noisy lorries or trailers, and altogether you have a thoroughly confusing time. As a 'teenager' you have things draped all over you, and not content with that, 'they' then get on you and expect you to let them stay there. What follows ranges from just about bearable to deeply appalling, depending on who 'they' are and the temperament of the horse.

It's probably true to say that the training towards Grand Prix starts with the handling of a foal. Kindness, firmness and consistency are the key words. It's always better (for the rider/handler) if a horse never finds out just how strong he is, because once this is discovered, it can potentially be a problem all through his life. Fighting with a horse is not something to start, so try never to put either of you in a position where a fight is likely – or if a fight is inevitable, make sure you win! If trust and confidence are lost at any stage, particularly with a young horse, it can be very hard to totally regain them.

Horses always have been, and always will be, horses – with a completely different way of looking at life from us. They are not affectionate in the way that we humans mean the word: what they care about is the acquisition of food and water, and equine company. Undoubtedly some horses are more people-orientated than others, but that's about it. Above all, they are not surrogate children or domestic pets: they are horses. They are much stronger than we are, whatever their age and size, and they don't

The first stage – just a few weeks old.

The second stage – three years old.

The third stage – mature.

Ideally the neck should come out of the withers at this angle. (Courtesy of Udo Haarlammert)

consider our wellbeing if they are anxious or afraid, they just react: they are purely creatures of instinct.

They don't differentiate between their own good and bad behaviour, other than by our reaction to it; they learn by habit and repetition what is expected of them. However, they can certainly differentiate between our good and bad behaviour and training, and react accordingly. It might sound pompous, but our responsibilities to them are enormous, in that 'the rider makes the horse'.

The Particular Horse

As we said at the beginning, we don't feel we can write about everything, and this includes a chapter on which horse to buy, beg or loan. However, age, temperament, willingness, trainability, natural talent, three correct paces, type, conformation, size and soundness all need very careful consideration – and, if at all possible, find a horse with the natural outline of the young mare in the picture (above).

Klaus Balkenhohl (top German rider, team trainer to the Germans and then the Americans) has commented that 'the best stallions are geldings'. They say that you 'ask a stallion, tell a gelding and discuss it with a mare' (this may not be quoted totally accurately, but the essence is there). Geldings don't have the raging sexual hormones coursing through their bodies that mares and stallions have, and because they don't, this can make them more reliable; this may be a generalization, but it is one that is backed up by many people's experiences.

Good, knowledgeable stable management and a good back-up team (trainer, groom, farrier, vet, dentist, saddler, physio, nutritionist) are essential elements in owning and riding a horse, whether or not the pursuit of 'glory' is something to which you aspire.

So assuming that you own a horse, or have access to one, let's get going.

2 Trainers and Training

To err is human, to forgive is equine!

(Unknown)

MIRACLES AND SHORTCUTS

Miracles come in two sizes: big and enduring; small and short-lasting. The big miracle is the horse – that in spite of having a body entirely unsuited anatomically for carrying a rider, he allows us on to his back and, even more amazing, mostly allows us to stay there! Then with the generosity of heart for which horses have been celebrated down the centuries, he tries his hardest to do the totally meaningless (to him) things we want of him – or not, and this is where the shortcuts come in.

People won't, or can't, wait to train the horse correctly, logically and patiently because that can take time. Chunks of training are left out, and the horse is just taught to perform 'tricks' – piaffe, passage, changes – without the rider establishing the basic, correct way of going and allowing the horse to develop progressively. Whilst it might look as if it works, the higher up the training ladder one goes, the more obvious the shortcuts become, as the horse often struggles to cope with the more serious demands in a willing and harmonious way.

The truth about shortcuts is that, once the horse has learned something incorrectly, it takes much time and effort to retrain; the process is inevitably flawed, and will often surface to disadvantage the rider at the most inconvenient moment – the original lesson will never be entirely eradicated from the horse's memory.

FINDING A GOOD TRAINER

One of the quandaries facing the horse owner searching for a trainer for themselves and/or their horse is to find a good one. There is probably no other industry so full of self-appointed experts or so many different methods, and quackery is rife. Word-of-mouth recommendation is probably the best way to find a trainer, as long as you back this up with some research into their credentials and the level to which they can train; although sometimes – actually quite often – long experience is more valuable than paper qualifications.

Look out for the rider/trainer at a competition whose horses look calm and confident in their work, concentrating on their rider who, in turn, looks part of the horse, with the partnership working in harmony. Mostly such people do well in competition – but whether or not they win, they are more concerned with how the horse actually performed. However, not all trainers can afford the time or money, or have the inclination, to compete, so looking only at competition records can unnecessarily restrict your choice.

When you find a trainer whose personality and philosophy suit you, then it is well worth staying with him even when things are not going so well – and there will be bad times as well as good. No miracles or shortcuts, just an appreciation and a deep knowledge of horses and their training, combined with an understanding of, and the ability to cope with, the pressures of modern sport. It is also very useful if he gets on your horse sometimes, firstly to feel what is actually going on, and what can be done about it; and secondly to demonstrate to you that your horse is actually capable of doing what is asked of him.

If your only reasons for going to the local trainer up the road are because it is cheap, convenient and undemanding, you will probably not further your knowledge very much. Nor will having a one-off lesson with someone famous, in the hope that they will somehow transform you and your horse into mega stars, help you progress if there is no particular input or effort from you. Top trainers can appear to work miracles as they often identify one aspect that can make a difference in the short term, and a fresh pair of eyes can be useful. However, for the longer term, you need someone who sees you regularly enough to know you and your horse, and is prepared to keep reminding you of the basics and what needs to be done.

A word of advice: young, 'thrusting' competitors don't always make the best trainers – first of all, they are young, so how much experience of training can they possibly have? Secondly, they are focused on competing on their own horses and those of other people; thirdly, they are often away competing; fourthly, they are probably much stronger physically than you, and can often get your horse to do things that you, quite simply, will not be able to achieve. Fifthly, they may be very talented riders, but they are not necessarily so good at explaining and passing on what they do without thinking to someone who can't do it. In fact, it can be that a talented rider can't explain at all what he does, or why he does something – he just 'knows'. This is wonderful for him, but it doesn't help you if you are his pupil.

Of course there are some exceptional young trainers out there, but age and experience really can count.

Most professional trainers and riders on the continent, and the best in the UK, have a broad, all-round knowledge of horse sport drawn from long experience in various aspects of the industry – and they bring that breadth, and the lateral thinking that it engenders, to their training, and have an appreciation beyond their own particular specialization of the ways in which horses can be trained.

Dressage is not a discipline that is taken up purely by people who can't do anything else: rather, it is embraced by those in pursuit of harmony and ease of performing with a willing partner of another species. These days, the emphasis in the world of sports training is more on trainers being coaches and enabling their pupils to progress, rather than just instructing them on what to do. This means a much more interactive process between coach and pupil, with the associated benefits to both from open discussion and a true understanding and awareness of the joint goals.

So whilst the trainer can train the horse and talk the rider through what is necessary, and spend endless hours explaining and re-explaining, in the end the rider needs to take responsibility for himself, his horse, and the training. Don't worry about asking for another, or clearer, explanation of something you don't understand; and don't agree that you do understand when, truthfully, you don't! There is no room for an over-inflated ego, or an over-inflated idea of your own competence, as neither of these does anything at all for you or your horse. Too much dependence on being instructed all the time can lessen the ability of the rider to think and feel for himself, which can, in the long run, be detrimental to progress – even though in the short term it is very helpful.

So an enquiring and analytical mind is a major advantage in unravelling the intricacies and challenges that lie ahead. Ask yourself, could I clearly explain what I know to someone else? When I ride alone, do I know what I should be doing and understand how to ask for it? Crucially, am I making it totally clear to my horse what I want?

- Whatever your financial state of affairs, regular training really matters, so find a way to afford the best you can.

Bear in mind that the top riders in the world, whether professional or amateur, consider that very frequent, preferably daily, training is essential. This isn't quite the contradiction it might seem, because training at this level is

NO SHORTCUTS!

There are not as many roads to Rome as people would have you believe – and there is definitely only one Rome.

much more about being a mirror for the rider's feel than instruction on how to ride.

Good trainers can immediately assess the way in which a horse has been trained by looking at

They say that a horse becomes more beautiful through correct riding. This is a four-year-old licensed stallion at one of Germany's state studs showing a beautiful uphill canter.

the muscular development of the topline – the neck, back and hindquarters – and also the muscle development of the forearm and the second thigh. By means of consistent and correct working of the neck and back muscles, the neck comes longer and more arched and the muscles underneath become soft and pliable; and the muscles in the hindquarters strengthen so that the rider is more supported under the seat. The horse's core muscles, those in the back and the abdomen, are part of the whole picture, as they support the back and allow the connection from behind to the front. If the horse's belly is dropped, then this is not happening. The result should be that the horse learns to carry himself, and his rider: he develops self-carriage, within his natural rhythm and balance.

An appreciation of the physiology and anatomy of horses, and the way in which they move – known as biomechanics – is essential to a rider's knowledge of the theory behind training. If you know how your horse's body is structured, you will be in a much better position to know what is possible and how to achieve it. An understanding of how the human body works is also good, and there are many excellent DVDs and books available that you can access to study these fascinating subjects in depth.

Some are beautiful anyway, of course! This three-year-old graded mare is owned by Udo Haarlammert; sadly, not all horses can attain this degree of beauty!

3 The Scales of Training

Horses lend us the wings we lack.

(Unknown)

THE GOVERNING BODIES OF EQUESTRIAN SPORT

The international governing body of equestrian sport is the FEI (Fédération Équestre International), of which the British Equestrian Federation (BEF) is part. The BEF includes all the FEI equestrian disciplines, represented by British Eventing (BE), British Show Jumping (BS), and other governing bodies for Vaulting, Endurance, Driving, Western, Reining and Para. British Dressage (BD) is the governing body of dressage in the UK.

These governing bodies each produce an annual rule book, and BD is no exception. The rules cover most eventualities and types of competition, and are required reading for competitors, as ignorance is no defence against transgression. It should always be the case that rules are interpreted by their spirit rather than by the letter, but these days, there's not much that hasn't been done before and thus it's covered by a rule somewhere! Being eliminated because you didn't read the rules is expensive, frustrating and unnecessary.

The *FEI Dressage Handbook* – Guidelines for Judging

The *FEI Dressage Handbook* is the definitive work for establishing just what each movement should be, its worth in marks, and the reasons behind the marks. It is more of a reference book than something to read from cover to cover in one go, but it really should be in the library of anyone who aspires to ride competitively or be a trainer or judge (*see* www.horsesport.org).

The FEI Mission Statement

> The object of dressage is the development of the horse into a happy athlete through harmonious education. As a result, the horse is calm, supple, loose and flexible, but also confident, attentive and keen, thus achieving perfect understanding with the rider.

This statement can be found at the beginning of the above book; below is the previous FEI definition, which we believe is worthy of attention even though now officially out of date, on the basis that most athletes are busy concentrating, trying their hardest and putting themselves under pressure when competing, and tend to look happier, or perhaps relieved, when they've finished – and this goes for the horses too.

> The object of dressage is the harmonious development of the physique and ability of the horse. As a result, it makes the horse calm, supple, loose and flexible but also confident, attentive and keen; thus achieving perfect understanding with his rider.

Happy athletes! Andreas Helgstrand (Denmark) and Blue Hors Matine.

Happy athletes! Isabell Werth (Germany) and Satchmo.

These definitions should probably be displayed prominently on a tack room (or bedroom!) wall – wherever horses are being ridden and trained!

AN ALL-ROUND TRAINING

In our opinion, a good basic training should be the start of every horse's education so that he is as prepared as possible for whatever he has to do in his life, whether this is dressage, jumping, hacking and so on. An all-round training – seeing and learning about the world, regardless of the 'career' that he, or rather his rider, will ultimately take up – can only be of benefit, and the concept known as the 'Scales of Training' gives definitive guidance as to how to achieve this. This concept is the golden thread that runs right

through the horse's training, in dressage from Novice to Grand Prix, the recognized scales being rhythm, suppleness, contact, impulsion, straightness and collection.

The Scales of Training

These scales have been defined over many centuries by celebrated Riding Masters, and we have tried to encapsulate the meaning behind these basic principles, or building blocks, so that the English terminology reflects the German words more closely.

These scales are the basis from which all dressage riders and trainers should work: if you keep to the scales you have a chance of training your horse well, and allowing his body to function optimally. (Elsewhere in the book you will come across their practical application, as

- Rhythm/regularity/balance   *Takt*
- Suppleness   *Losgelassenheit*
- Contact/connection   *Anlehnung*
- Impulsion   *Schwung*
- Straightness   *Geraderichten*
- Collection   *Versammlung*

Submissiveness/thoroughness (*Durchlässigkeit*) is the sum total of the above

they relate to the work needed to produce a well trained horse.)

Takt

Takt is the re-creation of the horse's natural way of going. It's the metronomic rhythm (the beat) of the walk (four-time), the trot (two-time) and the canter (three-time), and the regularity of the steps so that the horse can relax through his back and neck muscles and begin to carry weight over the hindlegs. Rhythm and regularity are interdependent with relaxation; a tense horse will be tight in the back and neck and will produce tense, uneven steps due to hollowness and loss of balance and he won't be in rhythm (*Takt*).

Losgelassenheit

The second concept, *Losgelassenheit*, or suppleness, is achieved through true relaxation, where the horse's whole body is free from tension and stiffness and can move in a regular, rhythmic, relaxed way and so is in a position to respond, without resistance, to the rider's aids. During this phase, the horse learns to work calmly and quietly; nervousness or tension will adversely affect his way of going and further training is unwise until this is sorted out.

Riding circles, serpentines, loops and transitions, as well as lungeing and riding over

cavaletti, poles or small jumps, can be useful to promote confidence and the gymnastic use of the horse's body.

Anlehnung

Contact/connection, or *Anlehnung*, is much misunderstood. Contact from the hand to the horse's mouth, whilst important, is not the whole picture. The horse learns to come from behind over a loose, swinging back through the

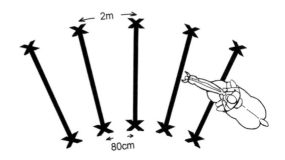

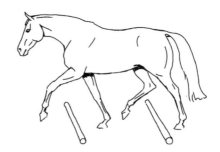

Trotting poles and cavaletti.

poll and jaw to the rider's hand, via the use of the muscles of the back and abdomen, and thus becomes connected from rear to front. This is the 'core' communication system between horse and rider. Without this total contact, there is a danger that this phase will be regarded as complete when, actually, there is only the look of it at the front end of the horse.

To achieve this connection, the horse needs to accept the rider's driving and restraining aids, via half-halts, so that the horse's mouth stays soft and closed, with a relaxed jaw, and thus can come into self-carriage. The horse no longer needs the reins for support and pushes himself 'to the rein' and accepts the contact.

Further correct training of the horse is not really possible without the above being in place.

Schwung

Schwung is the outward demonstration of the inner relaxation and shows impulsion plus swing, cadence, suppleness, balance, elasticity, elevation and ground cover (contained energy and activity). 'Impulsion', according to the FEI, is 'the desire to move freely forwards with actively pushing and over-tracking hindlegs'. This is only one part of the picture.

Geraderichten

Geraderichten, literally 'riding straight', requires all the above elements to be established before it is possible for the rider to truly straighten the natural crookedness inherent in all horses – and this is an ongoing process throughout the training.

Straight is taken to mean that the hindfeet track directly into, or over, the tracks of the forefeet with no sideways deviation. It is a continual process against the horse's natural inclination to be crooked and stiffen on one side more than the other, and requires both lateral

and longitudinal suppleness to counteract this.

To be 'straight' is also a requirement on any curved lines – through corners and turns, circles, loops, serpentines and so on – so that the horse is uniformly bent throughout his body in a way that corresponds to the lines of the movements and makes their correct execution possible.

The basic requirements for straightness are an even contact on both reins, with no resistance and with ease of flexion; the ears level and the poll the highest point, with no head tilting; the rider able to sit straight and square at all times; and circles, voltes and other exercises executed with equal ease on either rein. In other words, one straightens the horse through bending.

Lateral bend is where the horse is able to contract the muscles on one side of the body and expand the muscles on the other side, as on a circle or volte; and longitudinal bend is when the horse is straight through the length of his body from nose to tail (see Chapter 9, page 82).

Versammlung

Versammlung, or 'collection', is the culmination of all of the foregoing. Collection is the ultimate ability of the horse to carry weight behind and so lighten the forehand, due to the flexibility of the joints of the hindlegs, so that the elevation, cadence and expression of the paces can be developed through the most advanced movements to produce total self-carriage and harmony.

A horse that can be collected at will has reached the highest level of training: he has developed the necessary carrying power to carry out any, and all, requests from the rider without tension and with ease, suppleness and harmony.

This is also known as Durchlässigkeit (thoroughness/submission) – the sum total of the Scales of Training.

*Piaffe – ultimate collection (*Versammlung*): Alexandra Koralova (Russia) and Balagur.*

THE PHASES

Rhythm and Suppleness:
The Warm-up Phase

By nature, horses graze in herds and keep on the move for most of every twenty-four hours. These days, with few exceptions, humans keep ridden horses under artificial circumstances. Even if they spend some of each day in a field, the rest of the time they tend to be confined in small spaces that can cause them stiffness and tension in their bodies, however relaxed they may look.

For these reasons, it's very important that the warm-up phase of any work session is long enough to allow the horse to come into a natural rhythm and balance before being asked to work. Without this phase, the horse will continue to hold himself in tension, and suppleness will be hard to achieve. Hubertus Schmidt (top professional German trainer and Olympian), among many others of his peers, is passionate about the importance and benefits of the warm-up phase, as he feels that its omission is totally detrimental to the way in which a horse will work.

Although the emphasis in riding is on the horse going forwards, the first few minutes in the warm-up should be devoted to giving the horse time to re-adjust his balance to cope with the rider's weight. For this reason, many riders work their horses slowly and deliberately until they feel the horse begin to be comfortable in his balance.

The Cooling-down Phase

A note here about the cooling-down phase, which is just as important for the horse's well-being. Depending upon how hard he has worked, a few minutes in rising trot, long, deep and round, followed by some buckle-end walk (or some walk in hand) is a good way to finish, so the horse goes back into his stable in a relaxed frame of mind. (Of course, if you have the luxury of a horse walker, this could be used instead, but it is considerably less personal than completing the phase yourself.) The cooling-down phase is something that should be automatically incorporated into every horse's work sessions.

The nagsmen of old used to recommend a couple of miles of cool-down walk, with a loosened girth, at the end of a hunting day. In these days of horse transport such a thing is much less likely to happen, and it's easy to forget the mental and physical benefits of the cool-down phase.

Contact and Impulsion – Pushing Power

This is the second phase of the Scales of Training, and is the one where the rider develops the horse's energy by working the horse over the back from behind into a soft contact, using a well balanced combination of the driving and restraining aids (*see* Chapter 6, page 46). No aid should be too dominant or extreme.

Straightness and Collection – Development of Carrying Power

This third phase addresses the natural crookedness of the horse, and it is also where collection is developed by training the horse to take more weight behind.

Every horse is naturally crooked from birth, to a greater or lesser extent. This is not a problem to the horse until he is ridden when, eventually, such crookedness is likely to affect the spine and the back and can lead to physical problems. Also, if the crookedness under the rider is not dealt with (and this includes any crookedness of that rider), the energy potential from the hindlegs cannot flow in a straight line through the horse's body to the front legs, and therefore the horse won't easily develop the self-carriage that enables him to carry out the higher levels of training. (*See* Chapter 9.)

SUMMARY

One of the difficulties when riding and training is that some basic knowledge needs to be in place before most of the above can be understood in practical terms. Usually if the theory is there, and the intellectual concept is fine, it's the doing whilst riding that causes the problems.

Riders need to take responsibility for their own training and that of their horses. In particular, the rider should make some effort to absorb the theory and learn to sit correctly on the horse to the point where posture and position are automatic; that way, the brain is sufficiently unfettered to concentrate on the horse, the aids and the horse's reactions to those aids.

Every time a rider does anything with, or to, a horse, whether on the ground or in the saddle, a training 'habit' is formed. In the following chapters we would like to discuss ways to help make each training habit a positive one for all concerned.

4 The Rider

Horses see in black and white; riders think in grey.

(Unknown)

For the rider, natural aptitude is a help; natural feel and talent are more than a help; tall and slim are good; long legs and a not-too-long body are very good; natural balance and co-ordination, a brave heart, a good seat, excellent core stability and an analytical mind, coupled with emotional strength, complete the picture. In general, most successful professional riders have quite a few, if not all, of these attributes.

However, although all the above attributes are desirable, they are not essential. As many disabled riders have proved right up to Olympic level, it has as much, if not more, to do with will, grit, adaptability, determination and, as Lee Pearson says, a good seat. Riding – 'walking on horses' – has transformed the lives of many children and adults unable to walk on the ground, as they have learned to deal with the

Posture and position – Heike Kemmer (Germany) and Bonaparte.

Lee Pearson CBE (GB) and Gentleman (eleven gold medals and counting!).

movement the horse gives them and, as a result, have found their bodies 'unlocked' to a greater or lesser extent. Plenty of able-bodied but vertically or horizontally challenged people are competent riders. However, riders would be well-advised to consider themselves as athletes and deal with their own fitness accordingly.

POSTURE AND POSITION

Work on posture and position starts on the ground and is a daily 'work in progress' for everyone, since your posture off the horse will, not surprisingly, be reflected in your posture on the horse.

The Independent Seat

Later in the book we explain what we mean by an ideal seat, and such a seat is very important: without it, a rider is limited on a horse, and the horse is limited by the rider's ability. The basics are sitting upright and balanced, centrally on both seat bones, without needing the reins to retain your balance, at all paces and through all transitions, able to influence and control the

  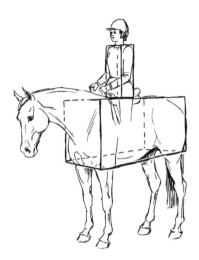

Perfect alignment.   *Vertical on horizontal.*

horse whilst so doing – in other words, perfect alignment!

Automatic synchronization of the aids is much easier with such a seat, and it enables a rider to judge more easily whether or not a horse is responding to the aids as he should. Coordination and balance in the rider are important to the development of coordination and balance in the horse.

Sports science is used across all the athletic disciplines, and riders are beginning to appreciate that they, too, need such information. This is because the rider – the human athlete – of whatever size, needs to be sitting in his own (vertical) balance on the equine athlete, who needs to be taught to rebalance himself (horizontally) as a direct result of the rider's weight.

Putting all the information and effort into the horse's welfare and training is only half the exercise; the rider has to make up the other 50 per cent.

Trainers need to learn to see and understand what is possible, physically, from their pupils, both human and equine. Endlessly yelling instructions about legs, hands, head, simply doesn't achieve this. The best coaches have a good understanding of the anatomy and physiology of their pupils, both horse and rider, so that help and guidance can be given and progress can be made towards the goal of a balanced rider on a balanced horse.

Associated activities such as the Alexander technique, pilates, yoga, bio-mechanical analysis and physio-therapeutic exercises can be added to the mix with great effect, as can self-help techniques, as described below.

Posture in Walk

Just watch the average person, whether rider or not, walking around the yard, the competition venue, the supermarket: are they upright, carrying themselves in balance, head up, chest out, using their arms, moving forwards positively, sound and level? Not very often. Most of us are fortunate enough to be able to walk without thinking much about it. However, changing the way you walk, even partially, can revolutionize your life and help your posture in the saddle.

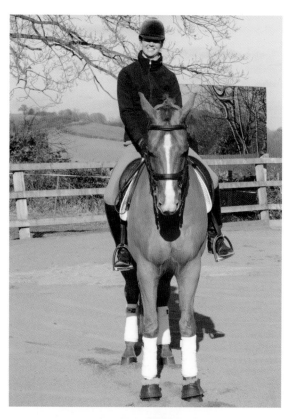

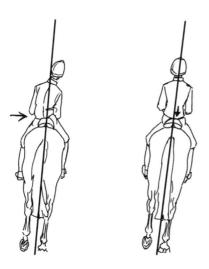

ABOVE: *Left – not straight, collapsed right hip.*
Right – straight and centred.

OPPOSITE *and* RIGHT *and* BELOW: *Before and after*
(specially posed!).

Relate this to what you require from your horse: upright, in balance, supple, using the joints, taking level steps, his weight evenly distributed over his feet, and moving freely forwards with energy, ease and the efficient use of the heart, lungs and musculature.

Make this new way of walking fit into your life – don't wait for the perfect week to arrive, but address the problem and navigate the solution: you walk anyway, so why wait? Approach it in the way you would hopefully introduce something new to your horse – gradually, or if you prefer, layer by layer.

Look at yourself in a full length mirror (wear tight-fitting clothes so you really see yourself). First, stand in your normal position – are you stooped or slouched? Then stand tall with your weight evenly over both feet, with hips and shoulders level, in balance, with the chest open, stomach muscles engaged and eyes looking straight ahead. Try walking a few steps like that, and then revert to your normal walk, and feel the difference.

Start looking at yourself in shop windows, arena mirrors, wherever you are, and notice how you walk.

As you walk, open the angle of the ankle so that you engage the muscles of your buttocks and legs, rather like the horse stepping through from behind. Then use your whole foot – from the heel, to the ball of the foot to your toes, trying to feel each toe individually, making sure you do this consciously every step you take. Feel the stretch and bend in your muscles and joints. Stabilize your pelvis (hips) by imagining balancing a glass of something you like to drink on each one (champagne works for us!).

Then open the angle from your ears to your shoulders (lengthen your neck), the chin slightly in, the head up and eyes looking forwards rather than down. Open your chest and drop your shoulders – and find out how much easier it is to breathe when you're like this.

Bend your elbows, put your hands in the ideal rein-holding position, and start using your arms

ABOVE: Walking, in a way often seen – look at the posture and the short stride (our pony, Ausden Quicksilver, looking on!).

RIGHT: Walking, in a way not so often seen – look at the posture and the longer stride.

as pumps, elbows going forwards and back as you walk. This can feel silly initially, especially in the supermarket, and it's hard to do it with something in your hands, but try it when you can. The more you pump, the more energy is released, and you also give your upper body a workout. Relaxation and rhythm (the Scales of Training) are the keys to good balance: holding yourself in tension is no more use to you than it is to your horse.

Put together, this will have you marching across the yard, balanced and energetic. The more you use your feet and pump your arms, the more speed, energy and power you develop – just like your horse when he works through his body and is connected from behind.

Finally, learn to breathe while pulling in your stomach (belly button to spine is quite a useful visual image). Initially it is difficult, so just do bouts of 10 to 12 seconds – and please remember to keep breathing. This engages your stomach muscles (core stability) and completes the system.

Technique and consistency are all-important, as ever. Done properly, or even done partially, this new way of walking should transform the way you look, how you feel and how you ride.

This is a rather 'one size fits all' approach, and not everyone will be able to do all of it – but just think of the benefits: recruitment of the correct muscle groups; alignment of the body; better balance; increased oxygen; increased energy levels; some relief from aches and pains (good for the back and hips); looking where you're going; positive and empowering self-confidence; and a more elegant aspect. Be proud of yourself, and look the part!

Just reading these words always makes us sit up and correct our slouchy posture; perhaps it will do the same for you!

● Thanks to Joanna Hall for her contribution to this section, *see* Further Information on page 172.

Lessons on the Lunge

Rider lessons on the lunge constitute the time-honoured, traditional way in which the continentals have always achieved their enviable position in the saddle. As the horse moves underneath you he needs you to move in rhythm and in balance on top of him so that he can move easily and in balance: regular sessions on the lunge, without reins and stirrups, on an established horse, well balanced enough to carry a rider on both reins, help you to achieve this. Also, this is the easiest way to learn about seat, weight and leg aids, without recourse to the reins or worrying about the steering!

Initially, exercises such as those that used to be taught to children – before Health and Safety regulations became an issue – are good, because they teach you some balance, and can remove any anxieties you may have about moving around on top of the horse. All the following exercises, or variations of them, help your independence on a horse:

● 'round the world'
● 'aeroplane' arms
● 'scissors'
● stretching the hand and arm up and then reaching down to touch the opposite toe with the fingers
● pulling your legs up in front of you, and behind you, as far as possible
● mounting and dismounting on either side of the horse
● stretching out fully forwards up the crest of the mane, or backwards until your head touches the horse's croup
● doing a controlled backward somersault off the horse

However, if you have physical problems it is important that you check with your physiotherapist before you do any of them, and make sure you discuss with your trainer which exercises you are comfortable doing, and which will be most positive for you. It is also essential to do them on a suitable horse, with the horse under control, with correct lungeing equipment including properly fitted side reins, in a confined space and with a knowledgeable trainer. Doing these exercises on a young horse, in the middle of a field, on a windy day is just asking for trouble!

Most horses can be taught – by someone who knows what they're doing – to lunge well enough to do a reasonable job in this regard. Also lungeing should be useful for the horse, insofar as it will help build up and/or maintain his fitness, and he will have to work in a rounded outline. Regular, consistent, informed work on the lunge is the best way forwards; the occasional bout of bouncing about on top of some poor unbalanced creature is a waste of time and effort, and is probably counter-productive.

RIDER WARM-UP

A warming-up period for the horse is a well-established part of training and, in general, riders are aware of how important this phase is for the well-being and the athleticism of their horses. However, riders seem to be much less convinced about a suitable (or any) warm-up preparation for themselves before they get on their horse, and in fact often pay only lip-service to the notion of preparing mentally and physically for training sessions or competition.

These days, however, there is plenty of scientific data to prove that riders who do prepare themselves have a distinct advantage over their rivals, and that time spent warming up leads to greater harmony between horse and rider. Actually there is nothing particularly scientific about this: if one of the two athletes involved in the riding process isn't warmed up, their stiffness and lack of mobility must have an

adverse affect on the other one. Think about it – if you've done some exercise, in general your body is energized and all the muscles are in good order for anything you'd like to do, including riding. Then imagine yourself (in this wonderful, relaxed, warmed-up state) getting on to a horse that's been standing in his stable for several hours and trying to get him to work with suppleness and thoroughness immediately. It wouldn't matter how well warmed up you were, the horse wouldn't manage until he was similarly warmed up.

It surely makes sense that the rider's body needs to be in an optimal state in order to ride his horse with maximum effect. When we compare other athletes where the main focus is on power, energy and stamina, we can see that the rider should be concerned with ease, relaxation and harmony, with the power, energy and stamina coming from the horse. *This is not going to happen if the rider is not as prepared as the horse.*

Being a good rider is about (in no particular order):

- elasticity of the muscles
- mobility of the joints
- a balanced, supple position
- achieving a balance between strength and technique
- knowing and feeling the rhythm of the horse
- using the seat, legs and hands to good effect
- leaving the comfort zone and still coping
- having total focus on what is happening
- dealing with his own tension and that of his horse
- reacting quickly and correctly

In order to maximize his own athleticism, every rider should consider the anatomical details of his own body so as to identify areas where mobility might be improved: the head and neck, sternum and ribs, muscles and ligaments, the sacroiliac joint, the pelvis, the legs and seat.

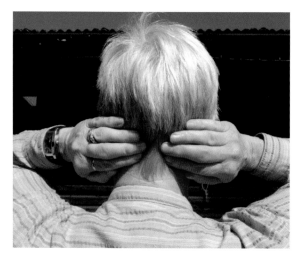

Occipital joint at the base of the skull (the rider's poll).

The Head and Neck

The head has primary control over the body – where the head leads, the body follows. A human's balance is crucially affected by the positioning of the head. If the occipital joint at the base of the skull, which connects with the first spinal vertebrae, is not free and mobile, the freedom of the rest of the body will be impaired. If the rider blocks this joint by looking down and sticking out his chin, the ability to turn the neck left and right will be minimized and there will be tension throughout the body. The pelvis will be blocked, as well as the joints of the limbs

You can make a direct comparison between the occipital joint in the human and the atlanto-occipital joint (the poll) in the horse: both need to be mobile and free from tension in order to function correctly and to be the highest point (except for the horse's ears!).

It can also work the other way up, to a certain extent. For example, it is important that the foot rests in the stirrup correctly, such that the leg hangs flat against the horse's ribcage, with the ball of the foot on the stirrup and the stirrup at right angles to the foot, and the knee slightly bent, so that the rider is able to move freely from the pelvis and the hip joints: if it does not, then tension will result all the way up through the body, and the ability of those joints to absorb the movement of the horse will be much reduced.

The Sternum and Ribcage

The movement of the horse is reflected in the rider, and vice versa. As with the horse, the ribcage and the thoracic spine (back) are much less mobile than the neck and lumbar (pelvic) areas. The ribcage can be likened to a corset that surrounds the body of both species and allows very little movement. Too much movement in these areas would destabilize the whole body and reduce the ability to cope with the pressures of riding, or being ridden.

If the rider is stiff in the spinal and pelvic areas, as is often evidenced in an inability to sit softly to the trot, the remedy is to mobilize these areas with exercises. (*See* Further Information on page 172 for information on exercise DVDs and equipment.)

Pinching the shoulder muscles.

Pinching the chest muscles.

Pinching the lower inside thigh muscle.

Muscles and Ligament Reflexes

Stress equals tension as a rule, and this cannot be overcome simply by using stretching exercises: more is needed. However, there are some seemingly minor exercises that, with daily application, should help with this (courtesy of Dr Meyners). Using your thumb and index finger, pinch the muscles that lift your shoulders several times, releasing between each pinch (or get someone to do this for you!). You can also pinch the chest muscles by pressing the thumb

Pinching the mid thigh muscle.

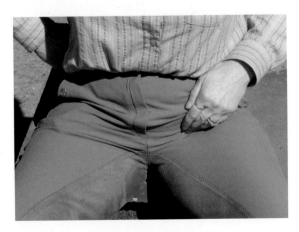

Find the anterior hip flexor muscles, and massage up and down, on both sides.

Pinching the top end thigh muscle.

into the chest muscle while the index finger is just into the armpit.

When you sit down and lift your foot off the ground, you'll be able to locate your anterior hip flexor muscle (the one that helps to lift your leg). Put it down again and, with the tips of your fingers, massage left and right across this muscle. Take care as this could be uncomfortable to begin with, but persevere as this will ease if done daily, and you'll find your hips much less tight as a result.

Sitting on a chair with your legs apart, pinch along the muscles from your pelvis to your knees to soften the tightness of these muscles. Again, don't go in too strongly at the start as you don't want to give yourself massive bruises!

The Sacroiliac Joint

This joint (where the base of the spine meets the pelvis) is very important as it allows a range of movements through the body: forwards and back, sideways left and right, up and down. Obviously, since everything in the body is connected to everything else, this joint is linked to the occipital joint at the base of the skull and can therefore either allow movement to flow through the body, or block it.

To help with this joint's mobility, lie on your back with one leg stretched out. Lift the other leg across the stretched one at as much of a right angle as you can manage and bend your knee, lowering that knee to the ground, whilst keeping your upper body flat to the ground. (This does get easier the more often you try it!)

The Pelvis

The pelvis is the most important part of the body, for the rider at least, and any stiffness in this region will adversely affect the rider's ability to influence the horse and will disturb the balance of rider and horse. Anything that stabilizes and strengthens this area is worth considering: pilates, yoga, wobble boards, the Balimo stool – all help to improve the core stability of the rider, and thus help the rider to use this area to maximum effect. (*See* Further Information on page 172.)

The Legs and Seat

In conjunction with the seat, the calf muscles in the legs are used to give leg aids to 'drive' the horse forwards. This only happens if the rider can open the legs enough from the hip joints, with help from the thigh muscles, so that the legs hang down softly on either side of the horse's ribcage, with the knees slightly bent and the heels lower than the toes.

Lie on your stomach with your legs straight and slightly open. Lift your lower legs up towards your buttocks, one at a time, slowly, holding the ankle with your hand, and then more quickly, repeating several times. In time, this helps the muscles in the legs to lengthen and shorten without cramping, and lessens the likelihood of them tightening, when what is wanted are relaxed leg muscles.

Another exercise that helps with being able to use one leg independently of the other, and also for improved balance, is to stand within reach of something to hold on to; lengthen your spine (stand up straight) without leaning left or right, and engage the muscles of your stomach (i.e. pull them in). Then lighten the weight on one leg by bending your knee, and stand firmly on the other leg. Eventually you should be able to do this standing free and lifting your leg clear of the floor with your knee even more bent.

The above is just a small selection of the sort of exercises riders can do off the horse to maximize their own athleticism on the horse.

Two athletes are definitely better than one!

Lifestyle Choices

From good posture comes good position and good body awareness, and these days there is plenty of information and practical aids to help overcome posture and position problems: a plethora of furniture – memory mattresses, pillows, cushions, underwear, back supports, shoes, boots, machines, balancing balls, boards and Wii Fit games – not to mention pilates, yoga, weight training and medicinal remedies. Just choose what you think is most relevant to you and your life.

Eating sensibly and healthily, just as you make sure happens with your horse, is also helpful for the 'fit for purpose' rider – never forget the adage 'fridge and cupboard pickers need bigger knickers'! You are, as they say, what you eat and drink – rubbish in, rubbish out – so smoking and endless coffee drinking, with pizza, pasta, burgers and chips each night, is not going to make you healthy, energetic and fit (never mind the alcohol)!

Theoretical Knowledge

There is so much theoretical knowledge out there – DVDs, books, magazines, lecture/demos, clinics, seminars, competitions (watch the best)! Go and find out for yourself what you can, discuss your findings with your peers and your trainer, ask questions, read some more.

It is not solely up to your trainer to educate and instruct you: finding out things for yourself is much more edifying, and the information is much more likely to stay in your memory. Blaming everyone but yourself because you are short of information and knowledge doesn't work any more (if it ever did).

Understanding the theory does make the practice easier – because you know the what, when, why and how. Equally, the importance of a schoolmaster horse on which to learn the feel can't be over-emphasized: you won't learn very much on a horse that simply doesn't understand what you want. You also need a trainer who has the experience of riding well to a high level, and who can explain the basics to you and, if necessary, give a similar explanation to the horse!

No one who knows would ever tell you that (dressage) riding is easy – but it is always fascinating and worthwhile. Beware those who are content with their level of ability, or think they know it all – keeping an open mind, and being genuinely humble, is all part of being a rider in the true sense of the word.

CORE STABILITY IN THE RIDER

What is 'core stability'? Is it important? Does it enhance athletic performance and reduce injuries?

The aim of core stability training is to effectively recruit the musculature of the body and control the position of the lumbar spine during 'dynamic' movements. Firstly you need to be aware of the importance of core stability; and secondly, you need to appreciate postural weaknesses around which a series of exercises can be individually designed to allow controlled, energy-efficient and well stabilized activities.

As with any fitness/exercise regime, it is sensible to start slowly, building up the intensity of the exercises gradually and progressively so that injuries are minimized.

The above applies equally to horses.

If you haven't exercised off a horse for a while, or ever, it's not sensible to go all out and give yourself aches and pains you didn't have before. 'No pain, no gain' is a common saying, and certainly you need to make efforts beyond your immediate comfort zone – *but* carefully.

A generalized core conditioning exercise programme will target the groups of muscles that stabilize the spine, pelvis and shoulders and control movement, shift body weight and transfer energy so that you can move your body and limbs, under control, with ease and a reduced risk of injury.

Although literature on sports activities often puts the emphasis on the abdominal and lower back muscles and those of the pelvic floor, in fact you should concentrate on a much wider group of muscles (approximately fourteen groups) that are contained within the length of the torso. These are the smaller, deeper muscles, rather than the larger, more superficial muscles that you can see; and this is where appropriate postural analysis is important, as each person will fall into a specific postural 'group', with considerations such as lifestyle, work, sport, age and any injuries taken into account.

Conditioning these muscle groups helps to develop the posture necessary to achieve and maintain balance and efficient movement, without effort or strain on any one area, especially the spine. All movements originate from the centre to the extremities – the limbs don't function on their own. For the body to work at its maximum capacity, the spine must be stabilized by the strength of the 'core' muscles at the front and back of the body, so that the person achieves full functional fitness and can cope with the demands on the human body that riding a horse presents.

There is plenty of information available on the sort of exercises that can deliver this fitness. A good and sensible first step would be an initial consultation with a personal trainer or physical therapist involved in sports rehabilitation and exercise programmes.

- Core stability is *not* some sort of passing fad: it is an essential part of the overall fitness for rider and horse that allows both to develop into the athletes they need to be for optimal performance.

(Thanks to Liz Launder for her contribution towards this section.)

5 Forwards/Downwards

*The horse already knows how to be a horse,
the art of horsemanship lies solely with the rider.*

(Unknown)

Forwards/downwards: these two words have been put this way round deliberately as the best philosophy is always to think, and have your horse thinking, forwards before adding anything else to the work.

If one studies the anatomy of the horse, it becomes apparent that the spine can only work effectively if it remains flexible and allows correct muscle development. When that is achieved, it is possible to bring the horse up and shorter without sacrificing the roundness and flexibility. This is why working the horse in the forwards/downwards stretched position generally has such a good and positive effect.

CORE STABILITY IN THE HORSE

Weak core stability in the horse is one of the major contributors to poor performance and an increased risk of injury, not to mention reduced stamina and poor balance. Horses without core stability usually have a dropped belly and a weak topline.

Conversely, therefore, a horse with good stability will:

- Perform correctly for longer and with more athleticism
- Work through from behind into the contact over a strong, supple back
- Develop correct musculature and look trimmer
- Develop good balance and posture (self-carriage)
- Move in an easy, powerful, coordinated way

Whenever a horse is worked the question should be, how can the muscles be strengthened and developed without losing their elasticity so that the horse can carry the rider on a strengthened back? So, riding a horse forwards/downwards is a concept that needs to remain with the horse from Novice to Grand Prix.

FORWARDS/DOWNWARDS

We sit on some of the transverse (cross-wise) processes (the bony protrusions) of the horse's spine, which attach to the longissimus dorsi (the main muscle in the back). When the horse stretches over his back and neck, forwards/downwards, these processes open up like a fan and form an arch, which frees the various longissimus muscles in the back to relax and contract without pressure, thus enabling them to strengthen. When we put the horse 'up', in a more advanced outline with the poll the highest point, the distance between each of these spinous processes closes up and thus the potential to make the horse uncomfortable and reluctant to carry the rider's weight is very real unless the back muscles have been made strong enough to cope. This is the point of the forwards/downwards method.

Forwards/downwards: relaxed, forward, confident, balanced, lateral and longitudinal bend – all the way up to Grand Prix: Isabell Werth.

topline, keeping the withers up. By nature, the forelegs are already more 'loaded' than the hindlegs, and the ultimate aim of training is to transfer some of that weight to the hindlegs so that the horse can come into self-carriage and become capable of collection, together with the necessary freedom of the shoulders.

Generally it's easier to show the forwards/downwards method to a just-broken horse, or to a young horse with almost no training, as there are fewer human-made resistances, and the young horse is more flexible in mind and body; however, it's never too late to improve the older horse's way of going through such training. A horse that is tight and hollow in its back can't build up 'good' musculature; only muscles with the good blood circulation that comes from being correctly worked over a relaxed back can build up progressively from the deep layers of muscle to

At the beginning of the warm-up, it might be neither desirable nor safe to go straight into forwards/downwards work. If the horse understands the work and is reliable and calm, then fine. If this isn't the case, then some warm-up in rising trot, and often canter, can be useful as the horse is more likely to want to stretch after a brief work session.

In addition, the conformation of some horses – those that are built on the forehand with a low set-on neck, and straight in the shoulders – mitigates against stretching forwards/downwards until such work has been completed. With such conformation, you still want the horse to stretch over the topline, but not so deep that they lose balance and topple on to the forehand; thus a smaller but genuine stretch is preferable.

It's important to understand the difference between a horse trailing its nose on the ground and being on the forehand, and one that is stretching forwards/downwards over the

Stretching forwards/downwards – reward, rest, relaxation.

GAINING THE HORSE'S TRUST

When a horse needs to see something, or when he is tense and upset, the first thing that happens is that his head comes up; in this way he can see peripherally round his body and can react, in a moment, to whatever bothers him. When we ask a horse to work forwards/downwards, we take away that possibility, so trust and confidence in the rider is an essential part of the horse's willingness to put himself in a position that makes him vulnerable.

the surface muscles we can see, and for this, forwards/downwards can be most beneficial.

Many riders ask how they can get the horse to do the forwards/downwards stretch, and expect an answer that can be put into practice in minutes. Sadly, it's not as easy as that; it takes patience, time, knowledge, experience, feel and constant attention to achieve it.

The exercise is more easily done on bent lines, as the horse finds it easier to go into both reins. As soon as the horse gives and drops the neck, the rider's hands should be ready to allow this. In the early stages it can be necessary to give the horse a very long rein so that he learns to trust that the contact won't be snatched back and he will feel able to seek out the contact.

Speaking of snatching, you don't want the horse to snatch the reins out of your hands – if this happens, resist the snatching briefly and then repeat the sequence to get him to take, or follow, the contact forwards/downwards, calmly and smoothly.

Ultimately you want the horse to go to the contact: he yields, you soften, and he stretches down more, reaches the contact, you soften, and he stretches down more. In this phase, the rider should not force the horse into an artificial outline by the hand alone, as the horse will immediately use the muscles underneath the neck and can become strongly resistant to the rider's hand. The right reaction is achieved when the horse passively lets go of the neck at the withers.

Ideally, stretching should be done in all three paces, alternating with taking up the contact for a few strides, then releasing again, so that there is a willingness from the horse to accept and follow the contact and the changing outline.

Another important factor is that the horse should be ridden forwards from behind, but not hurried; the horse's natural rhythm and balance should be maintained so that the horse doesn't 'run away' in front – that is, run through the reins, lose balance and fall on to the forehand. Using half-halts is therefore useful and necessary, however basic they may be at this stage. The energy from the activity of the hindlegs should be constant, but not more than can be given with the hands.

The rider's attention should be focused on whether or not the horse shows any inclination to stretch forwards/downwards so that this can be immediately encouraged. It is more difficult to establish this method with a horse that has been wrongly trained for some time. In this latter case, it is useful to bend the horse and make him laterally submissive, by putting the stretching of the neck into a more exaggerated inside position. This can have the consequence that the neck becomes too short briefly. The outside rein is held passively and with a forward inclination to keep the inside bent position until the horse submits, which can, initially, go against previous advice and take more than a few seconds. When the horse yields, the rider must immediately give forwards with the inside rein to encourage and allow the horse to stretch correctly into both reins.

Most horses will stretch forwards/downwards of their own accord after some time spent on this exercise. If the horse wants to hollow away from this lateral bend, with hindlegs trailing,

Pessoa training aid: top, loose fitting; bottom, more closed setting – note the adjustments at the shoulder and stifle. Jane Brook's 'Summer Story'.

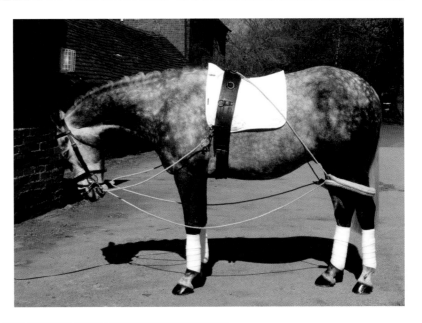

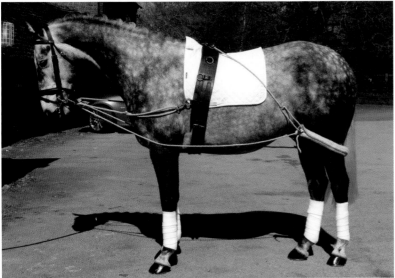

the contact needs to remain secure but never hard or pulling backwards, and should be constantly backed up by renewing the inside leg aid until he comes softly back into the contact with a rounded back.

- The hands, used alone, to 'make' an outline or to 'force' the horse to lower in front, do not achieve anything useful or lasting.

It can often be the case that it is not possible, initially, to use inside leg to outside hand. Sometimes lateral aids – the inside leg and hand or the outside leg and hand – are necessary until the horse gives to those aids. Sometimes it is necessary to use the right leg and hand on the left, or vice versa, depending upon the problem that has presented itself.

If you have a horse that needs some

rehabilitation, it can be useful to lunge using a Pessoa training aid (Google 'Pessoa', and lots of sites come up) prior to riding. This lungeing should be done with great care and over time so that the horse gets used to the new way of using himself without stress. The usefulness of the Pessoa is that the horse quickly finds the most comfortable position for himself, and any deviation from this position means he fights with himself against the Pessoa and not against you. With this work, the horse will soon find that stretching forwards/downwards makes life more comfortable, and should more easily volunteer to go in this way.

How deep a horse will stretch forwards/downwards differs from one horse to another – and in any event, the individual's natural way of going should be paramount. If the horse is on the forehand, and leaning against the rider's

---

ROLLKUR/HYPERFLEXION

Riders often confuse the correct forwards/downwards stretching with pulling the neck in tightly, sometimes into the chest, to a deep outline well behind the vertical, which has been forced on the horse and from which he can't escape.

This achieves a tense, anxious horse, blocked in the back and totally behind the aids, and thus incapable of the work being asked of him without resistance somewhere in his body. Used long term, or for long periods of time, this is often typified by a broken neck and, much worse, a broken spirit or a permanently angry horse. However, this doesn't stop some riders, and there has been much written about it in the media.

This method, and it is a method, is called 'hyperflexion' or 'Rollkur'. It has caused a lot of controversy over the years, and the FEI has, finally, come up with a declaration with regard to its use in the public domain, as follows:

Fei Press Release
Lausanne (Sui), 9 February 2010

Fei Round Table Conference Resolves Rollkur Controversy

Following constructive debate at the FEI round table conference at the IOC Headquarters in Lausanne, the consensus of the group was that any head and neck position achieved through aggressive force is not acceptable. The group redefined hyperflexion/Rollkur as flexion of the horse's neck achieved through aggressive force, which is therefore unacceptable. The technique known as Low, Deep and Round (LDR), which achieves flexion without undue force, is acceptable.

The group unanimously agreed that any form of aggressive riding must not be sanctioned. The FEI will establish a working group, headed by Dressage Committee Chair Frank Kemperman, to expand the current guidelines for stewards to facilitate the implementation of this policy. The group agreed that no changes are required to the current FEI Rules.

The FEI Management is currently studying a range of additional measures, including the use of closed-circuit television for warm-up arenas at selected shows.

The group also emphasized that the main responsibility for the welfare of the horse rests with the rider.

(This is just the resolution, and will be ratified and added to the FEI Rules in due course.)

Many would say that this doesn't go far enough, but different horses need different methods of training for a myriad of reasons, and it's all about degree.

hands, half-halts should help to get him off the hand again and come into a light contact. The rider should never try to put every horse in the same mould – each one is different.

Furthermore, after ten to fifteen minutes of this sort of stretching work, the horse needs to be allowed to put his head and neck in a free position with which he feels comfortable, as it is tiring for his muscles to be in the long, deep and round position for long periods. This is quite normal, especially for a young horse, so don't imagine that all your hard work has just been ruined! It is also a good indicator that it might be time to finish the work session for that day.

It can be perfectly acceptable that a horse is sometimes behind the vertical: look at the whole picture and see if the back is swinging, the hindlegs are engaged, the balance is good, the ears are floppy and relaxed, the eye is quiet and the rider is able to change the frame, up and down, in and out, with ease, and that there is always a connection from behind to the contact into which the horse is working. Young or inexperienced horses often go momentarily behind the vertical as their balance changes, and this is not a sin. Always have regard for the overall picture.

Correct forwards/downwards riding enables the horse to carry the rider's weight without damaging his back.

LOW, DEEP AND ROUND

In the foregoing sections, what we call forwards/downwards is the technique known as 'Low, Deep and Round', or 'LDR': it is not the controversial method known as 'hyperflexion' or 'Rollkur' (*see* panel opposite).

When a horse is truly on the aids with a contact that he has sought, rather than one imposed on him, he is able to use his body and actively step under and work over his back.

Gerd Heuschmann is a German veterinarian, who trained as a professional rider, well known

for his views on how young horses should be ridden so as to develop correct musculature and prolong active and healthy lives. We have taken these excerpts from Dr Heuschmann's book *Tug of War: Classical Versus 'Modern' Dressage*, as they mirror the views we have put forward above:

> Riding forwards and downwards does not mean – and this is something that is often misunderstood – that the horse should run on to its forehand. It only means that a young horse that has not yet developed the necessary muscles to carry a rider is given the chance to 'carry' its back (including the thoracic abdominal weight – the trunk – and the rider) by moving with a head/neck axis that is as stretched out and forwards/downwards as possible, while maintaining a swinging, natural back.
>
> … a young horse moving in this posture learns quickly to allow the pushing power of his hindquarters to flow through the back, over the poll into the rider's hands. This is the only way to develop the indispensable connection from back to front.
>
> … the loose, relaxed back is the decisive prerequisite for a natural motion sequence in all three basic gaits, releasing the long back muscle (the *longissimus dorsi*) and allowing the rider to sit comfortably.

Forwards/downwards stretching is only one part of the whole training of the horse, albeit one that plays a central role throughout the levels. It can make the difference between a horse that can function naturally in an optimal way, and one that is forced into a 'shape'.

It is an effective test of the correct training of any horse that he is willing to be placed in any frame or position, whether high and collected or long and low, without resistance. The converse is an indication that all is not well with the training. Our aim is to achieve what Christoph Hess calls 'an inner silence', where horse and rider are mentally and physically relaxed and focused on each other.

6 Aids in Action

Knowledge of the aids, and how to apply them, is really essential if you intend to ride and train your horse: aids are the basic tools, and both horse and rider should have a good understanding of them in order to facilitate their mutual communication. However, knowing about them, and applying them practically, are not always the same because what is theoretically achievable is not always so simple on top of a moving horse.

Although you would think that aids should be the same for everyone, in practice they are quite individual in timing, application and reception. An aid is given, received, acted upon – the rider 'says' something, the horse 'responds' and the rider 'listens' to his horse. However, like any communication system, it is only as good as the initiator and receiver understand it, and in this regard it has to be the rider who gives the aids well enough to make as sure as he can that the horse understands what is being asked.

One thing to remember is that the one with the brains (presumably the rider) should be in charge and in control of the one with the brawn (the horse). Where things go wrong is when the rider is unsure and/or timid, and the horse becomes confused and takes over the decision-making. One way to counter this is to make sure that you ask your horse to do more or less the opposite of what he offers (unless, of course, you want what is offered!) – so if he wants to tear off in trot, you ask for a slower, more moderate trot; if his idea of canter is to stick his head in the air, or on the floor, and

tank off, find a way to achieve a slower, more considered canter. This way, psychologically, you become the herd leader and everyone is happier – even the horse, as his brain is not set up to make decisions when he has a rider on his back, and his instincts of fright and flight are seldom what are required. He is not a machine (if you want one of those, ride a bike!) and he should be a willing and enthusiastic partner, so you are not trying to dominate him so much as, subtly, stay in charge!

'Aids' mean just what they say – they aid and give direction – so when you've given them, let the horse carry out the request: don't interfere and confuse him by continuing an aid past the point where it's necessary, because this leads to resentment and resistance as the horse feels there is nowhere he can go without being continually nagged.

THE VOICE

The voice is one of the most underrated aids, and can be used to excellent effect when working with horses, whether being handled or ridden. For lungeing it's essential for the horse to react to the voice, the body language of the handler, the interaction between these two elements, and the whip. Further, the voice is indispensable when first riding the young horse as it is already familiar and can be used to reward, encourage, calm and admonish when necessary. This is something to be carried on throughout training, and it shouldn't be forgotten even at the highest levels – think how pleasing a kind word can be, whoever you are. An over-keen or over-anxious horse, always wanting to be forwards, can be reassured with a quiet tone and soothing voice.

Horses are not deaf, in fact their hearing is much more acute than ours; find a definite, firm but pleasant tone that has some authority in it, and differentiate, with your voice, for an upward transition, a downward transition, walk, trot and canter. In Europe, *galop* or a derivative is used for canter, so initially, 'canter' or 'canter on' might not be understood by imported horses.

What voice aids are there? It's not the words really, but the tone and the constant repetition of a phrase or word that the horse learns to associate with an oft-repeated action. Horses will generally respond by halting if 'whoa', or 'stop', or 'halt' are used regularly; most European horses respond to 'brrrr' or 'prrrr'.

Pushing your horse back away from you in the stable, or using the word 'back' (*zurück* if the horse is German!), teaches him that he can, and should, back up when asked, and is a way to teach him not to invade your personal space unless you allow him to do so.

Tones, whether loud, aggressive, hesitant or soothing, create a reaction in your horse. Probably the most important thing is to be consistent in the words and tones you use, so that your horse can rely on you and gain confidence and trust. The Germans use the word *konsequent*, which translates very well into English – horses need riders and handlers to be consequent and consistent, so that all know where the boundaries are, mounted or unmounted.

This leads on naturally to praise: it's all too easy to castigate your horse for not understanding, being wilfully 'naughty', difficult, stupid, obstinate or just plain stroppy! With the exception of the first one, which is your fault, none of the others is really something horses do. We humanize our horses'

reactions – in other words, we put our human interpretation on how the horse is behaving.

Contrary to popular belief, horses do not get up every morning having plotted overnight the ways in which they can frustrate and thwart their owners! Horses can certainly be bright, intelligent and fast learners, but conceptual thought is beyond the best of them: they live in the moment, and generally, what humans perceive as bad behaviour is often a learned response to previous bad or wrong handling and training, or as a defence mechanism against incorrect riding.

So, praise. However big one's ego, it's always nice to receive thanks or praise, so when a horse does something really well, it can only be good to reward him. Lots of people feel that the only way to give such praise is to lean forward, clasp the horse round the neck, and/or nearly beat him to death with heavy pats on the neck. However, you can't do that mid-test, or even mid-work, without losing continuity; and not all horses appreciate such heavy slapping on the neck (and if you're leaning forward embracing your horse, this could be the moment when something spooks him and you're on the floor!).

Doubtless most of them learn through repetition that this is, in fact, a 'good thing', but horses are sensitive creatures and a discreet pat on the neck or a light scratch at the base of the withers is just as effective and can be incorporated into a momentary giving of the inside rein, which can relieve tension and stress in both horse and rider.

What works really well is to use a soft tone of voice, together with the light pat or scratch, so that the horse learns that this is praise. Later on, you can phase out the voice and keep the light touch.

BODY LANGUAGE

This happens involuntarily between creatures of all species and is something that horses pick up on immediately. By your position, posture, tension (or lack of it) and breathing, you influence your horse. Equally, of course, your body language can contradict what you imagine you're telling him, so it needs careful consideration. Just think about what people like Monty Roberts advocate – they use appropriate body language when dealing with a 'difficult' or frightened horse, and the horse reacts accordingly.

Together with the voice, body language is a most important aid, and horses also react to your body language, tension or relaxation, when you are riding them.

Horses use body language themselves to indicate their intent; learn it well, and your communication and response can double in value, whether you are riding or handling them. Importantly, you can better anticipate situations that might endanger you and your horse. Horses see and hear things that we don't; they have much magnified instincts, with fright and flight top of the list. Be alert to how your horse responds to everyday happenings, and make sure that he's confident that you're the herd leader and will 'protect' him; otherwise he'll make instinctive decisions that you could live to regret!

- You 'speak' to your horse every moment that you're with him, so make it count! Horses 'speak' to us and it's up to us to 'listen' to them. They are very sensitive and intuitive; we should remember that, and use these qualities to our own advantage.

THE INTERACTION OF SEAT, LEG AND HAND

Traditionally, the percentage use of the seat, the leg and the hand is 80 per cent seat, fifteen per cent leg and five per cent hand. Most of us would say – 'I wish!' – but just watch Hubertus Schmidt, Isabell Werth, Steffen Peters, Andreas Helgstrand, Kyra Kyrklund, Christine Stueckleberger, Carl Hester and other top riders, to see this in action.

You could say that you need to 'surround' or 'contain' the horse within the aids, so that horse and rider are totally concentrated on each

The interaction of seat, leg and hand – Christine Stueckleberger (Switzerland) and Aquamarin.

The focus bubble.

forwards, and the amount of actual driving will depend on many factors – the aim being to have the horse respond to the lightest and slightest of aids. This applies equally to the restraining aids – using technique rather than brute strength, so that the harmony between horse and rider can be developed to the point where all aids are virtually invisible to the onlooker.

The weight, seat and leg aids are more to do with driving, and the rein aids with restraining. It follows that the combination of all four makes it easier for the rider to regulate the paces – the tempo (speed), the rhythm (beat) and the outline (frame) of the horse: in other words, to communicate with and control him.

- Permanently strong aids make for an insensitive horse, and will eventually ruin him.

other, rather like being in a bubble that excludes everything outside the partnership.

Note that although we've devoted separate sections to weight, leg and hand aids, they are not really divisible – all are needed together in order to influence the horse to carry out what you've asked him to do.

Aim always for light aids, but don't be afraid to make them stronger when required to ensure a reaction, bearing in mind that a lighter aid should follow immediately to reinforce the point. Strong aids, constantly applied, simply deaden the horse's reactions and are exhausting for everyone concerned – the rider, the horse and any onlookers. Light aids, on the other hand, demand the horse's attention – so whisper rather than shout.

The Weight Aids

Just by sitting on the horse, the rider is using weight aids. That's why it is so important that the rider has a balanced, independent seat, sitting on both seat bones (if you can't find them, just sit on a hard chair with your hands underneath your buttocks, rock backwards and forwards, and the hard bones you'll feel on the back of your hands are the seatbones). The next step is to find 'pelvis neutral', tipping neither forwards nor backwards: this is the basic position. Think about wearing a belt on your breeches: in pelvis neutral the belt is centred and parallel to the ground; if the pelvis is tipped up and forwards, the belt buckle will be raised; if the pelvis is tipped back, the buckle will go down.

There should be no space between the rider and the saddle (imagine being firmly Velcro-ed to the saddle!), so that the rider is always in contact with the horse through the seat (unless you're rising to the trot, of course!). The added bonus is that maintaining such a position in the

Driving and Restraining

'Driving' and 'restraining' are terms that can suggest a very domineering approach to riding, and indeed such aids are often used in this way. Basically, we think that driving should be taken to mean the use of seat and leg to ask the horse to go forwards, or more

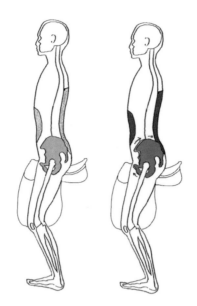

Pelvis neutral. Tilting pelvis – up and forwards, down and backwards.

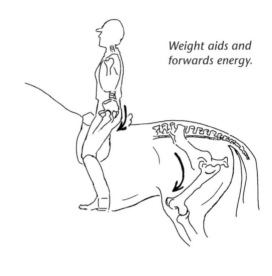

Weight aids and forwards energy.

saddle requires much less physical strength than a seat that is out of balance, which requires constant adjustment.

The rider's buttocks should be relaxed and spread all the time; tightening the buttock muscles, particularly in downward transitions, is to misunderstand what's required.

The seat (which is shorthand for the rider's whole body) could be described as the trunk of a strong tree, carrying the weight of its branches, which are your legs and arms. The branches can act independently of one another, or together, but always rely on the support from the seat. Strength and control of the core muscles are really essential to the retention of a correct position and the ability to give appropriate aids. (*See* 'Core Stability in the Rider' at the end of Chapter 4, page 38.)

In order to swing with the horse's back, which lifts and sinks as the horse moves forwards, the rider tightens and relaxes the abdominal and back muscles, which in turn control the movement and direction of the pelvis. To send the horse forwards from halt, or to create more energy, or for an upward change of pace, the rider should sit tall

through the sternum and engage the abdominal muscles (pull the belly button in towards the spine as the sternum lifts); the back muscles engage in conjunction with the sternum and the abdominals, and together raise the pelvis and push it forwards; at this point you need to be ready to follow the horse's forward momentum and pick up the rhythm of the forwards motion. Although this might sound like a big movement, it isn't: you could say that you momentarily increase the tension in your body and this converts into a forward energy without leaning forwards or backwards.

To decrease the pace, or make a transition downwards, you need to relax that tension without collapsing your posture; what you do is restrict that forward push by not pushing forwards! This process is difficult to describe adequately in words because so much of this is to do with feel. How do you 'make' yourself walk, run, skip, halt – could you explain what you do? To a certain extent, you decide to do these things and they just 'happen'. The use of the muscles you need to engage in order to ride effectively is more or less involuntary in the sense that you just learn what works, without necessarily understanding the 'how' of what you do.

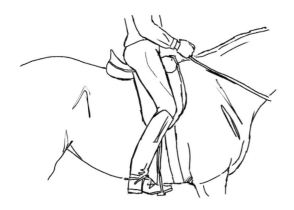

Ideal leg position – side view.

The Leg Aids

Your legs are attached to your body at your hips; the hip joint is at the top of the leg and is then connected into the pelvis (we all tend to speak of hip movement when actually we mean pelvic movement). The rider should be aware of using the whole of the leg – or more specifically, the inside thigh muscles, the knee, the inside muscles of the calf, the inside ankle joint and heel. The knee has a light contact with the saddle; the ankle joints should be supple and loose; the ball of the foot just rests gently on the stirrups and the heels are relaxed downwards (heel lower than the toe).

It is very important that the rider finds the right stirrup length so that he can stay with a relaxed and comfortable leg position, without losing his own balance, at all paces. Stirrups that are too long make you stand on tiptoe, with raised heels and locked knees, which in turn means that your lower legs won't hang loosely down either side on your horse – and you will not have a secure balanced position. If the rider's legs are used correctly, the horse's movement is deflected and absorbed in conjunction with the pelvis, abdomen and upper body so that the rider can sit to the horse's movement. If a rider's head nods, it's usually an indication that there is stiffness somewhere in the body.

If the toes are turned out, this generally means that it's the back of the calf and heel that are being used, which in turn means that the rider is gripping with the legs. This restricts the quality of the leg aids that the rider can apply, and also hinders the rider's ability to sit.

With a horse that's slow to react, the leg pressure can be increased, returning to a relaxed position when the aid has been successful. In other words, keep the leg on, or use a couple of quick, sharp kicks, or tap with

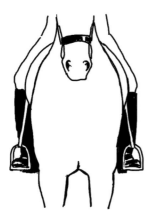

Correct leg position – toes point forwards.

Incorrect leg position – toes turned out, with the back of the calf and the heel gripping the horse's ribcage.

the whip – you need a forwards reaction – but be ready for a more extreme one than you hoped for! Almost any reaction is better than none, as you can temper your aids to the desired reaction when the horse has got the message. In general, leg aids are best timed to be applied within the rhythm of the horse's movement. To be precise, the correct leg aid should be given when the horse's inside hindleg is about to leave the ground. It's up to the rider to make the horse obedient to the leg. We want to end up with very light leg aids to get the horse to go forwards.

Leg aids can be made with both legs together, or separately. Forward aids tend to be both legs together; sideways aids, and aids for circles and turns, involve both legs but doing separate things. The inside forward driving leg is positioned at the girth; the outside supporting leg is a hand's breadth further back, more or less passive, and is there to prevent the quarters from falling out; however, this leg can also be used as a sideways driving aid in conjunction with lateral work (*see* Chapter 12).

There is also the sideways driving inside leg, which is taken slightly back to facilitate the sideways movement; this works in conjunction with the outside supporting leg, which can also be actively used to maintain the forwardness, if necessary. The rider should be insistent that the

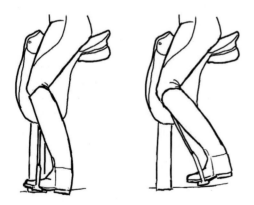

Leg on the girth. Leg behind the girth – supporting and/or sideways driving.

horse really does step sideways; if not, then the aid needs to be increased or aided by the whip or spur. The horse should willingly go away from the sideways driving leg, but first make sure that the horse understands that he should yield to the rider's leg, otherwise he will push against the leg pressure. The horse needs to learn that when the aid is given, and then the pressure is released, he should go sideways (*see* 'Leg Yield' in Chapter 12, page 105).

It can be that a horse is reluctant to go forwards; in this event, believe it or not, sending him sideways away from the inside leg, and thus getting him moving, is often one of the best ways to translate this reluctance into the forward obedience you were seeking. Again the horse must first understand the aids; just trying to shove him over with the leg doesn't work very well.

The Rein Aids – The Hands

On the whole, problems of contact start the minute most riders take up the reins – and although this is a generalization, it is often not far from the truth. Humans are hand orientated and tend to concentrate on things that they can see, so it follows that a major preoccupation of many riders is the position of the horse's head and neck rather than keeping to the correct principles of training – that is, working the horse from behind to the rein.

Holding the reins correctly is important for the maintenance of a good, feeling, consistent contact between rider and horse. The fingers should be closed round the reins with the thumb on top (slightly arched) – *see* illustration opposite – without the hand closing into a tight fist (so, with a little hollow remaining within the fist).

There are two essentials: first, that the thumb isn't flat and tight; second, that the ring finger and the little finger remain closed, but not tight or unyielding.

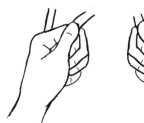

Correctly held reins (snaffle), from above.

Correctly held reins (snaffle), side view: thumbs relaxed, ring and little fingers closed.

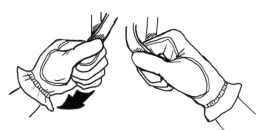

Wrist turned in to achieve flexion.

RIGHT: **The default position.**

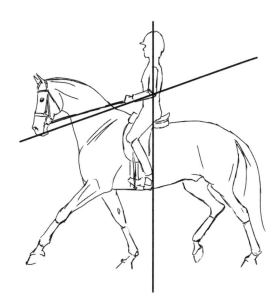

Rein aids are mainly given with the fingers (closing around the reins with more or less intensity, but always staying shut) and wrists (turning in to achieve flexion and then returning to their default position), in conjunction with relaxed elbows – not with the whole arm and shoulder – and elasticity of the contact comes from this.

Elbows and shoulders should be relaxed, with the elbows resting comfortably by the rider's sides, and the hands either side of, and just above, the withers, with a straight line from a bent elbow through the rider's forearms and hands to the horse's mouth. This is the 'default position', which then makes a connection to the bit.

The muscles of the forearms should be relaxed and soft – if the hands are turned over so that the backs of the hands are uppermost, the fist tends to be clenched, the forearm muscles become tight and unyielding, and there is usually also tension in the elbows and shoulders. The reins should not be taken across the withers but held one on each side of the withers.

The rider's hands should act in a controlled, sympathetic way, indicating within the already existing contact what the horse should do. The outside rein controls the speed (tempo), flexion, bend and the outside shoulder; the inside rein takes care of the softness, initiates bend and flexion to help the suppleness, indicates the turns, and controls the inside shoulder.

Thinking about the reins as sticks that are always used to push the bit forwards, but without losing the contact with the mouth, can be a useful visual image.

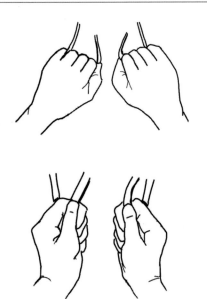

Hands: Top left – incorrect, the back of the hands uppermost, with tight thumbs.

Top right – incorrect – hand across the withers.

Bottom left – stiff wrists, with flat, tight thumbs.

An inconsistent rein, far from being kind, is just as unpleasant for the horse as a tight rein because the horse feels nothing in his mouth and then, when the rider takes up the rein, the bit is suddenly activated, sometimes with considerable force, which causes discomfort, tension and resistance. The tight rein is usually tight because the rider is nervous of losing control, or uses the reins to balance himself, or is trying to make an outline – and a tight rein is often one which is pulled back towards the rider's body, and this equally causes discomfort, tension and resistance. In both cases, there is no possibility of 'feel' between the rider and the horse's mouth.

As a general principle, the contact should only be taken up as much as the rider can drive to the rein, to keep the horse forwards and in balance. In simpler terms, don't take more at the front than you can drive from the back. According to Ulla Salzgeber, for every centimetre you shorten the reins in front, the horse will shorten his stride a corresponding amount with the hindlegs, *unless* the energy and throughness from behind are maintained. However, if you relax your shoulders and move your elbows, you can achieve the shortening

without making the contact tighter or stronger, and without affecting the stride. Some horses respond to a lighter contact than others, some like a firm contact – it's a question of feel.

Sensitivity and feel are crucial to keep a horse's mouth equally sensitive and free of resistance. Too much pressure on the mouth – and the 'mouth' comprises corners, bars, tongue, soft palate, jaw – leads to defence mechanisms from the horse which include opening the mouth, hanging the tongue out, putting the tongue over the bit, grabbing the bit, dropping behind the bit, coming above the bit, carrying himself incorrectly so that the neck is supported primarily by the under neck muscles, and a back that is hollow and stiff.

Swishing the tail and/or grinding the teeth are sometimes suggestive of an underlying muscular problem, or anxiety, but can also be simply an indication of intense concentration. Some horses just plain swish and grind! The overall picture will normally tell the story.

At the beginning, anything that encourages the production of saliva (sugar, mints, horse cubes) can only be good so that the bit is viewed as 'a good thing' by the horse. However, such treats need to be used judiciously so that the horse doesn't expect them all the time and become pushy or aggressive. Quite a few riders give a titbit at the start of a ride and again at the end.

In a correctly ridden horse, the reins remain elastic – a rubber band, almost – with only as much tension as will keep them taut – not loose, or in a loop or tight – to establish the connection from behind over the back to the rein. The slow, measured give and take (or squeeze) is like a continuous dialogue and is always used in combination with forwards-driving aids.

The rider's responsibility is to be sufficiently balanced in his own position that he can keep the contact as consistent and quiet as possible at all paces and through all transitions. However, the actual length of the reins will vary according to the level of training, the movements being ridden, and the pace in which the horse is working, and should be of a length that enables the rider to give aids with minimal interference.

The amount of work the hands do will depend on the level of the horse's training: the lower the level, the more frequent and obvious will be the giving and taking to cope with the changing balance and rhythm.

The reins should be taken up by means of the fingers closing round the reins like a sponge being lightly squeezed out; if the horse doesn't react to this, then the wrists need to be slightly turned in towards the rider's stomach to increase the momentary restraining aid, in conjunction, as ever, with the elbows. Pulling

backwards with the arms is not acceptable as this provokes the horse's resistance, together with a hollowing of the back, and a trusting, confident, forward feel of the contact will then be hard to establish.

THE ARTIFICIAL AIDS

Artificial aids include whips, spurs and auxiliary reins. There are many styles and variations of all three, and most have a useful role to play. They are, however, supposed to be used judiciously to back up the rider's aids in a refining way, and not as punishment for something the rider has failed to impart to the horse, or as a prop for an unbalanced rider incapable of giving correct aids.

In the real world, spurs and whips are often used as substitutes for correct riding. However, there are also occasions when a horse does need to be rebuked, and then such aids should be used as sparingly as possible and immediately there is the need; horses do not associate cause and effect if separated by more than a very few seconds, so quick retribution is essential. Losing your temper, however, and taking it out on the horse is not a useful way to train.

Seat, leg, hand – Emma Hindle (GB) and Lancet.

Auxiliary reins (draw reins, for instance) have their place in experienced hands where rehabilitation is necessary, and to keep both rider and horse safe from extreme behaviour.

Just to re-emphasize the point: strong aids lead to stronger and stronger aids, which lead to the misuse of spurs and whips, not to mention draw reins and other similar artificial aids, to force the horse into submission. There is a place for such artificial aids, but not used day to day in a way that avoids learning to train your horse properly.

THE PACES

Walk

It's relatively simple to sit on a horse in walk because the walk has no moment of suspension (there's always one leg on the ground); the walk just has activity and energy. The sequence is hindleg, foreleg on the same side, other hindleg and then foreleg – sequentially one after the other and four clearly separated steps.

The movement of the rider shouldn't hinder the horse's rhythm but should regulate the speed of the walk and, in conjunction with the leg aids, produce bigger, rounder, longer steps that cover the ground or, shorter more elevated steps, depending on the walk required – medium, extended, or collected. The more relaxed the horse is over the back, the more clearly the different walks can be demonstrated.

When the rider sits correctly as already described, his legs will rest softly against the horse's ribcage and he will be able to feel the ribcage swing in towards his legs alternately, from side to side; this is effectively the leg aid for walk.

A supple contact, with the hands following the neck movement forwards into a bigger, more open frame, will produce a correspondingly bigger walk. This walk develops from medium walk into free walk on a long rein – that is, with some contact retained, so that the horse stretches down into the rein. Extended walk is very similar but the horse should draw forwards into a more defined, less deep, 'light and steady' contact. Collected walk needs to come from behind with shorter steps into a shorter frame and not from slowing the walk and pulling the horse into a short, tight frame.

Walk on a loose rein – holding the buckle end with complete freedom of the neck – is something for the beginning of the warm-up phase (if safe to do so); as a reward and relaxation in the work phase; and at the end of work or the completion of a test, after the final halt, and during the cooling-down phase.

Over-riding, or using excessive aids, will disturb the horse's natural way of going. Riders often tend to try to make an outline from the front by shortening the reins but the effect this has is to shorten the steps of the hindlegs, hollow the horse's back, and restrict the neck and shoulders – any or all of these can lead to the clear four-beat rhythm being compromised.

Walk is quite fragile – it's easy to create faults in training that will be hard to eradicate, so it's generally considered sensible not to overdo work in walk with young or inexperienced horses, and certainly not to over-collect them and risk losing the purity of the four-beat rhythm.

The idea is that the rider provides the frame, but the horse takes the contact: in other words, the horse comes into the contact because of the rider's aids, and when the rider releases the rein to lengthen the frame, the horse takes the contact forwards and downwards. That's the aim. This is something which has to be trained, and which the horse needs to learn; *it doesn't happen by magic.*

Stimulation via pressure on both sides of the ribcage should cause the horse to lift his back and, with the help of his abdominal muscles, also lift the ribcage. For the rider, this creates the feel of having the horse's back up underneath the seat – sort of filling out the hollow, if that helps create a visual picture.

Lateral Walk

This is not a walk you want – it is a bad thing!
Very few horses have a naturally lateral (or
pacing) walk: it is almost always the result of
tension and incorrect training. Viewed from the
side, the horse doesn't keep to the usual
separate footfalls of hindleg, foreleg on the
same side, then the other hindleg and then the
other foreleg. Instead, both legs on one side
swing forwards and back together so the walk
becomes a two-beat pace – just like a camel's.

Horses with a huge natural over-tracking walk
often find collected walk very difficult, and it is
often such horses that can develop an incorrect
walk if sufficient care is not taken during
training. If the rider only thinks of restricting the
horse in front with the hands, trying to obtain a
shortened frame, and doesn't allow the correct
movement of the head and neck, a lateral walk
often results.

Interestingly, dealing with such a walk usually
involves employing lateral work (*see* Chapter

ABOVE: **Medium walk.**

BELOW: **Extended walk.**

*Free walk on a long rein (above); free
walk, at the buckle end (below).*

12), as the horse tends to revert to the correct four-beat sequence when going sideways, so leg-yield, shoulder-in, half-pass, travers and renvers are all very useful. However, it's very important that the rider keeps a light but supple contact, and that the hand never overrides the seat and leg aids.

It is possible to 'cure' a lateral walk, but it tends to resurface whenever tension or an over-tight rein returns.

Trot

In the trot the legs work in diagonal pairs (a two-beat rhythm) and in between each diagonal there's a moment when all four feet are off the ground – 'the moment of suspension'.

There are four sorts of trot – working, medium, extended, collected – to which riders can sit or rise, depending on the situation and their own ability. However, it would be extremely unusual to rise in collected trot. The rhythm and tempo should remain the same throughout all the trots; it's the length of stride and frame that varies.

Rising Trot

There is no need to 'stand up' and 'sit down'; a forced pushing up out of the saddle is incorrect, quite unnecessary and usually followed by an unbalanced, heavy return. The rider should be lifted by the horse's swinging back and forward energy, returning softly and in balance to the saddle. It is sufficient when the seat, depending on the suspension of the horse's trot, comes a few centimetres out of the saddle and the return should be careful, aided by support from your thighs, so that the rider sits down in the saddle with loose, swinging hips, and good core stability.

The sitting phase of rising trot is the moment when the rider can give a driving aid if required.

The leg aid starts in the thigh and goes through the leg into the calf, ankle and heel, as previously explained, so that the aid is given without the leg and heel coming up and back, with a subsequent possible loss of the stirrup. In fact, with your leg in this position, you give the aid with the inside (flat) of your calf and, when necessary, the inside of the ankle and heel.

The weight aids are transferred via the seat bones on to the horse's back. Quite often, just the mere fact of the rider putting weight into the saddle, in the sitting phase, is sufficient to drive the horse forwards. It is important that the rider remains in a balanced position, that is without a chair seat, fork seat, or otherwise unbalanced or crooked seat.

The arms and hands keep a soft, constant connection to the horse's mouth, through slightly bent elbows, hands with the thumbs on top, to the horse's mouth.

With riders who take their balance from the reins – that is, the horse's mouth – it is visible that the reins go up and down as the rider does so, and there tends to be a backward pull on the reins at the same time; this produces a negative reaction in the horse, and as a result he is often not willing to go forwards because he has learnt that the rider will bang on his back, pull him in the teeth, and won't give a positive forward driving aid. Balancing like this on the reins is not only incorrect, it is also counter-productive.

These remarks apply equally to sitting trot.

Sitting Trot

Most important in sitting trot is the rider's ability to swing and absorb the horse's movement. Only when he has learned to adapt to this can he influence the horse with subtle and considered aids, without losing the suppleness of his seat or the relaxed position of the legs. Obviously the weight aids are now permanently influencing the horse's back, and

'Variations on a theme' – often seen but not what's needed! Top left – collapsed seat; behind the movement. Top right – chair seat. Middle left – fork seat. Middle right – fork seat, hunched shoulders. Bottom left – in front of the movement. Bottom right – hollow, stiff back, lower leg held back.

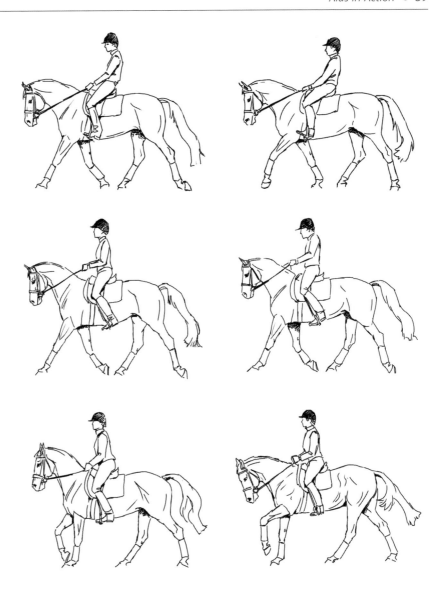

the rider must be able to choose whether or not to use a stronger seat aid in conjunction with the leg aids. It's important to keep the sensitivity of the horse by using aids that are as light as possible, and used only when necessary; momentarily stronger aids should only be used if the horse ignores the aids. To be clear, both legs are used together at the girth.

● The rider is always responsible for how the horse accepts the aids.

Canter

In the canter the legs work as follows: outside hindleg, inside hindleg and outside foreleg; inside foreleg (known as the 'leading' leg). It's a three-beat rhythm with a moment of suspension after each full stride.

There are four sorts of canter – working, medium, extended, and collected; the rhythm and tempo should remain the same throughout all the canters; it's the length of stride and frame that varies.

A good forward working trot.

*Andreas Helgstrand
and Blue Hors Matine:
an elegant, effective
position; a forward,
energetic collected trot.*

*Medium trot:
Carl Hester (GB)
and TMoviestar.*

In the canter, the horse should be positioned slightly to the inside (flexion and/or shoulder-fore) over the leading leg in order to keep him straight, because otherwise the quarters are invariably to the inside (the horse is wider behind than in front, and is also innately crooked). Both hands need to be following forward enough to allow the horse's necessary neck movement in the canter without relinquishing the contact.

Traditionally it is said that the rider should put the inner hip forward to weight the inner seat bone, both in the canter depart and in the canter itself. This is, of course, quite true. However, if you position your legs correctly from the hips, just by putting your outside leg a hand's breadth behind the girth, you will have your inner hip forward and this is sufficient. However, this will *not* be the case if you swing your outside leg back from the knee and leave your hips as they were in trot. *This is really important.*

It is equally important that the rider maintains the 'canter' position of the hips and legs throughout the canter work, otherwise the horse is quite likely to return to the trot when he feels the rider's position change to 'trot' (when the rider's hips are parallel again).

The rider should actually sit in the saddle during all three phases of the canter – in other words, he shouldn't come out of the saddle at any stage, because the horse will no longer be being influenced and will make his own decision as to whether or not to keep cantering! The movement of the canter should be taken up by the lower back and hips of the rider, and the upper body and the legs should remain as quiet as possible – grinding away with the body, or moving the upper body forwards and backwards, is not useful or productive.

However, having said that, the rider should find that a slight forward inclination of the upper body aids the forward momentum of the

Carl again, this time with Uthopia – all the qualities that canter should have.

canter and eases the facility with which the horse's back can come up under the rider's seat.

The canter aids should be repeated only when the horse either slows or loses forward energy; in other words, he should continue to canter until told otherwise, staying in front of the leg. The canter strides should be long and ground covering, not short and choppy, and must, above all, maintain the three-beat rhythm and the moment of suspension. Horses are very often particularly crooked in the canter – the positioning mentioned at the beginning of this section needs to become a total habit every time the horse canters in order to keep him straight, and also so that his inside hindleg can come under the centre of gravity, and energize the next step he takes. Do make sure, however, that your reins are an appropriate length – too long a rein becomes a hard rein as the rider takes his arms back in an effort to retain control.

A slight forward inclination of the rider's upper body in canter – following the movement.

RIDING THE ARENA

Corners

In an arena, there are four corners. They can be completely ignored, as riders often do, or they can be used as part of the training process to ride good circles and as a set-up for lateral work on the long sides.

Viewing each corner as a quarter circle works well. With less experienced horses, the corner is really just a curve, with a couple of straight strides at A or C; however, as the training progresses, the corner becomes a smaller and smaller quarter circle, from 10m right down to 6m for an advanced horse.

At risk of stating the obvious, tighter corners are easier for the horse to do in walk than they are in trot or canter. So the size of a corner that's possible for a novice horse in walk would not be possible for the same horse in canter, whereas an advanced horse should be able to cope with a very similar sized corner in walk, trot and canter.

A corner is a turn, which is an extra reason to learn to ride good corners, as many dressage tests have turns, rather than curves, in them. If you imagine having to ride through a curved tunnel at each corner you will get the idea of what should happen. Each step through the tunnel is part of the turn or corner.

An exercise that reinforces the above, and makes it easier for horse and rider, is to make a transition from trot to walk as you approach the first corner, then ride a quarter turn in walk with your inside leg at the girth, and a passive outside leg just behind the girth to stop the quarters from swinging out. Flex the horse to the inside (not neck bend), allow that flexion with your outside rein, and ride through the corner. Take up trot, walk before the next corner, and repeat. If you find that your horse is too onward bound to do this easily, add a halt after the walk transition before each corner, then walk, turn, perhaps halt again if necessary, then walk and trot to the next corner, and repeat.

Alternatively you can ride a square, which has the advantage of being much smaller than riding the full arena between corners. Referring to the mathematics of the arena (*see* Chapter 15), decide at which markers you want to make your square, which will give you four corners, and ride through the exercise as before. If you don't have an arena, set up a square using jump

Corner.

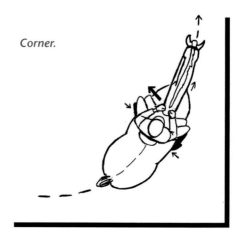

LEFT: *The horse's whole frame follows the line of the bend through the corner in trot (imagine the tunnel).*

RIGHT: *The horse's whole frame follows the line of the bend through the corner in canter.*

poles, cones, barrels, whatever you have to hand, and start riding corners and turns.

When the above is going well, and your horse understands what you want and is waiting for your aids, try replacing some, if not all, of the actual transitions with half-halts, so that you can trot through the whole exercise. So that would be half-halt before the corner, set up the positioning and ride through the turn, half-halt coming out of the corner to control the tempo if you need to, ride to the next corner, and repeat.

These exercises work well in canter, too, but are much more demanding for horse and rider, so perfect them in walk and trot first.

Circles

If you can ride corners, circles become easier because you and your horse have learned how to make turns. Chapter 15 gives you the maths on circle sizes and where in the arena they can be ridden, depending on the size of circle you choose. Always start big and easy, and gradually reduce them to smaller and less easy.

● The first thing to remember about circles is that they are totally circular. So you can't ride a circle that incorporates a corner, which is a turn as we've established, and any straight strides after the marker mean that no way will your circle be circular!

With the maths in place, visualize the diamond shape within a circle within a square (*see* diagram overleaf). Then, with the flexion and half-halts already sorted from the corner exercise, you ride from tangent to tangent. Bend your horse evenly round your inside leg, with a slight flexion according to the size of the circle, the outside leg behind the girth guarding the quarters from swinging off the line of the circle, and the outside rein controlling the speed, the degree of flexion and the outside shoulder.

You should be on each tangent point for only one stride, otherwise you will have introduced a straight line into the circle. A circle is really a continuous turn until you're back where you came from, so you need to keep turning, otherwise a straight line will creep in.

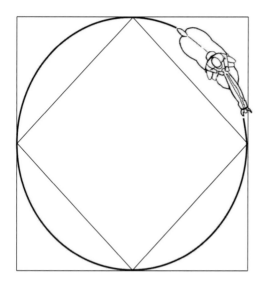

Diamond within a circle within a square – the horse correctly bent on the line of the circle, touching the four tangent points.

Drifting through the outside shoulder is the death of many a circle and turn – as is stepping out of the circle line with the hindlegs, usually as a result of too much neck bend, or falling in on the circle with the horse's weight on to the inside shoulder.

Being able to ride corners and circles means that you have achieved the essentials of having your horse bent round your inside leg, upright to the outside rein, flexed with the inside rein, supported by the outside rein and staying straight on the curved line of the circle, or through the corner. This also means that you will be able to ride centre lines and diagonals with ease, but much more to the point, you will have the correct set-up out of the corner, or off the circle, for lateral work, extensions and pirouettes.

INSIDE LEG TO OUTSIDE REIN

Much has been said and written elsewhere about inside leg to outside rein, as if there isn't an inside rein or an outside leg doing any work. This is far from the truth. The outside rein's main functions are to control the pace, the speed of the pace, the degree of bend or flexion, and the outside shoulder; in other words, to control and channel the power from behind.

Acceptance of the outside rein is, however, something that comes with training. With a young or inexperienced horse, the more active rein is often the inside rein because its action is more direct, guiding the horse with a steady contact to bend and turn, supported, of course, by a more passive outside rein.

The rider's outside leg often fulfils a guarding, or passive, role, but is no less important for that. Without that leg in place, horses would be very inclined to swing their quarters away from the influence of the rider's inside leg, rather than engaging their inside hindleg and powering themselves forwards. At the beginning of training, the rider needs to teach the horse that

he should move away from the pressure of the inside leg rather than barge into it. As just mentioned, this is where the outside leg has a guarding function.

It is often the case that both the rider's legs are involved in sending the horse forwards; if that is the stage at which the training still is, then the forwards way of going should predominate, and everything else needs to wait until that is completely understood.

In the early stages the rider should use whichever rein or leg he needs to at the time, and forget any 'rules'.

● Ultimately, however, the horse should be upright into the outside rein, round the rider's inside leg, with a soft inside rein taking care of the flexion and bend, supported or directed by the outside leg.

At that stage, inside leg to outside rein can reign supreme!

7 On the Bit = Contact = Connection

A good rider can hear his horse speak to him. A great rider can hear his horse whisper.

(Unknown)

CONTACT

Many people misunderstand this subject, so this chapter is our attempt to explore the concept and perhaps make it clearer.

The three expressions are interchangeable, and mean much more than that the horse has an arched neck at the front. The horse is connected within a circle of energy forwards from the hindlegs over the back (the bridge), via the rider's seat and legs, first to the poll and then to the mouth, and back again. It is the suppleness throughout the body, and through the poll, that gives the softness and lightness of the contact; this is when we can say that the horse is truly connected, or on the bit, or to the contact (and this applies just as much in halt as in motion) – and in balance.

Definition

The following quote is from the German National Equestrian Federation handbook:

On the bit = contact = connection; this applies just as much in halt as in movement. Debbie McDonald (USA) and Brentina.

Contact is a soft and steady connection between the rider's hand and the horse's mouth. While training progresses, the horse should be ridden from behind into the elastically yielding hand. The contact will then be even on both reins when riding straight ahead, and a little stronger on the outside rein when riding on a circle.

To achieve a contact, the reins may not be moved backwards. Contact has to be the result of well developed propulsive power. When forward driving aids are applied the horse has to move forward into the contact.

… contact does not mean that the horse may lie on the rider's hand. He must find his own balance and not try to use the reins as a 'fifth leg'.

… to establish a contact the rider must bring the horse's hindlegs further underneath his body. This stretches and elasticizes the neck and back muscles … through this swinging back the propulsive force generated by the quarters can now be transmitted forward to the horse's mouth. The horse submits to the energy coming from behind; he flexes in the poll and champs the bit – in other words he is 'on the bit'.

Poll High

When the horse is in this state, the poll should be the highest point of the outline, with the nose marginally in front of, or on, the vertical, viewed from the side. Viewed from the front, it should be just possible to see the headpiece of the bridle and one, perhaps two, plaits (not more) behind the headpiece. This is more difficult to achieve with mature stallions with big crests, or with horses not trained this way from early on, and quite frankly, not many riders/trainers achieve this ideal, as you'll see in the photographs; however the principle remains.

The young stallion again, and the Scales of Training in action.

Trust and Contact

Perhaps the place to start is with the establishment of trust – that the horse trusts the rider's aids and, more specifically, the contact between the rider's hands and his mouth; that he trusts you'll be consistent and fair and not ask of him anything unreasonable or unprepared. You can't 'make' a horse trust you any more than you can make a person trust you.

● Trust always has to be earned.

A lot of the evasions put up by horses are to do with problems with the contact. This is undoubtedly 'man made', and it's worth taking a good deal of time and effort to ensure that your horse is accepting of the contact as early as possible. This requires a good, balanced position in the saddle, from which deliberate aids can be given to the horse, and he in turn needs to be sufficiently balanced to receive and act on them.

We are talking about a horse that is free from any physical problems – if the latter exist, then they should be dealt with before asking the horse to work.

ESTABLISHING BALANCE

Horses are, in the vast majority, perfectly well balanced on their own. Even the big, gangly ones manage well without a rider, and foals learn early to cope with their legs and bodies. It's certainly true that some horses are better balanced, naturally, than others, but this generally results from some defect of conformation and such horses still manage.

Where balance can become an issue is later, when they are ridden, as they then have to adjust their balance to accommodate the rider and learn to cope with the changing balance of that rider. Helping the horse to re-establish his natural balance should be one of the rider's main concerns because, if this is all right, the rest of the work comes much more easily.

Although we've said, many times, that riding forwards is paramount and that certainly does apply overall, it's always necessary to think about the horse's balance. It's often the case that initially the horse will need to be ridden quite slowly and with small steps, using plenty of walk, halt, walk transitions, until he feels less worried about the weight he is carrying and has regained his own balance; only then is it all right to ride him forwards. Riding a horse powerfully forwards as soon as you get on can cause him great anxiety because he is neither mentally nor physically ready to cope with the balance.

This readjustment to his balance is something he has to do each time he is ridden, and the slower work and transitions give him the time he needs. Most top riders understand this and start their warm-up in this manner, whatever the level of the horse they're riding.

Some horses are naturally well balanced, and others acquire balance through training, but it's always worth giving balance the careful consideration it deserves.

● Balance is a small word, but one of the biggest in terms of training any horse and rider.

PROVIDING A FRAME

Basically, the rider provides a frame for the horse by taking up the rein enough to feel his mouth – the length of rein will depend very much on his length of neck and his body – and then asks him to go forwards into the contact, flexing at the poll and relaxing the jaw. He rides the horse on to the contact; he doesn't 'put' the horse on to the bit, as this latter suggests something static and done by the hands alone. 'Seesawing' left and right – as is so often seen – does not, and cannot, achieve a consistent

Compare with the photograph on page 65 – a square halt, but off the aids, above the bit, hollow.

contact, because there is never the steady rein that is needed.

What mostly happens initially is that when the rider takes up the rein, the horse often refuses to move at all: he throws up his head, hollows his back and generally resists any pressure in the mouth. Seldom do things go as smoothly as some books would have you believe! (If it were as easy as that, we'd all be able to do it.)

If your horse hollows against the contact, try very hard not to pull back or use your hands to try to re-establish it; instead, keep your hands quiet and 'there', and ride forwards until he drops back into the contact – wait, and give him time to do this. It is crucial that this isn't done only with the hands: your core muscles are involved to stabilize your seat (so that you can't be pulled forwards out of the saddle) so you can ride forwards from this position.

● When the rider takes, the horse gives; when the rider gives, the horse takes.

In this 'give and take', it shouldn't be a sudden grab of the rein followed by dropping the rein, as the horse feels either too much pressure or none. The idea is to do the 'give and take' within a consistent, firm but elastic feel on the reins; your fingers remain closed around the rein, but the wrists and elbows allow the necessary elasticity. This usually teaches the horse something vital: that when he yields to the pressure of the reins in the poll and jaw, the rider will give the reins enough to allow him to do as he has been asked. Should he resist the contact, the pressure from the rider's seat, legs and lower back are momentarily increased to reinforce the message that he should 'give' before the rider does so.

The reward for the horse when he gives to the taken rein is that the rein is relaxed, and the rider becomes more passive. This is really important so that the horse learns that a quick reaction from him is rewarded by an equally quick reaction from the rider – and this is how sensitivity to the aids is built up. The communication between rider and horse is a constant to-ing and fro-ing of asking, allowing, doing and rewarding, with the aim of doing less and less with the resultant relaxed, calm state on both sides.

If the horse tilts his head to one side it is often because there is stiffness at the poll, or one of the hindlegs is not stepping under the body with the same length of step as the other one. So it's reasonably safe to say that only when the horse is soft and relaxed at the poll and stepping under equally with both hindlegs in an energetic manner, can he be truly on the bit.

This takes time and patience, and the horse is highly likely to put up a fight in the sense that he will come up with all sorts of evasions. This is the reality and, given that horses are unlikely to have read this or any other book, there does come a time when you have to persist, and make it clear that this is something that is going to be insisted on.

● The best advice we can give is that you should persevere, as long as you are sure you're playing your part correctly.

TIPS

The rein on which the horse tries to hang, whether inside or outside, is the one which should be softened and given, time after time, so that he learns to go to the rein but not be supported on it. Making that rein the one that you hang on to merely strengthens the muscles on that side of the horse's neck, ensuring that the poll is stiff and the jaw resistant.

Horses that lean on the rider's hands can be dissuaded in two ways – if you don't pull, they won't! Walk–halt–walk and trot–halt–trot transitions are very useful; in the early stages, you will find you need a strong aid to insist on what you want, but release the aid very quickly, repeating if you need to, using your seat and core muscles to help, until the horse obeys lighter and lighter aids.

With a horse that runs through the rein, that is to say, doesn't respect the rein and barges on regardless, you need to halt immediately he gets strong; flex him and make him soft via the inside rein, walk on again, and repeat as necessary. Transitions, walk, halt, walk, should do the trick but only if you're quick enough to halt him again within one or two strides. Repeat as often as it takes so that he goes forward to the rein and not through it.

If the hindlegs are engaged and the horse is moving forwards well, with a good, consistent, steady contact and with the help of transitions, he will come into the contact more or less automatically.

Lateral driving aids – using the leg and hand on the same side – rather than inside leg to

Against the hand.

*Above the bit, off
the aids, off the
ground!*

outside hand, can be most useful on the less accepted rein, as can work on curved lines.

SUMMARY

Before you can move on successfully to higher levels of training, it is really crucial that this stage – that is, having your horse 'on the bit', with all its connotations – is truly understood and established. 'On the bit' means that your horse allows you to organize his body (and brain) to the extent that he accepts being pushed forwards, via your seat and legs, to the contact (hand). In this way, he learns to stay in balance with his contained energy at your disposal.

Your legs hold him to the contact and make a frame (outline) inside which he needs to move (whether this frame is long or short) and he needs to follow the contact within a varying frame without losing the connection. When you give the rein forwards, the test of being 'on the bit' is that he follows the contact to the end of the rein. All this presupposes that the horse is submissive, soft and light in your hands and remains so.

● Very often, with horses as with life, what works is the opposite of the obvious!

ABOVE THE BIT/ BEHIND THE BIT

It is to be hoped that the phrases 'above the bit' and 'behind the bit' are self-explanatory, especially with the accompanying pictures – and we've all seen horses demonstrating these extremes. Quite often one sees horses going around quite calmly with the neck and head stretched out, in a long frame, often with the quarters either trailing or simply not active enough. However, although both horse and rider may be quite content with this approach, it does rather preclude being able to perform any movements that require collection or extension, or lateral or longitudinal suppleness.

Both with the above, and the more extreme versions of 'above the bit' or 'against the hand' where the horse more closely resembles a giraffe, the whole horse is likely to be stiff over the back and unable, or disinclined, to work from behind to the contact in a good, supple, connected way. Within these extremes there are further degrees of extremity, as evidenced by the pictures.

The usual remedy involves going back to basics with some forward riding into a definite contact – but not one that holds on grimly, especially on the stiffer side – backed up by driving aids which initiate the connection from behind. Circles are good here, as are transitions, but the 'cure' takes time and patience while the horse adjusts to the new way; his 'reward' is that it gradually becomes easier and more comfortable for him to carry his rider.

Tense, against the hand, tight in the neck (broken neck), not supple at the poll or relaxed in the jaw – not a chance to flex this horse.

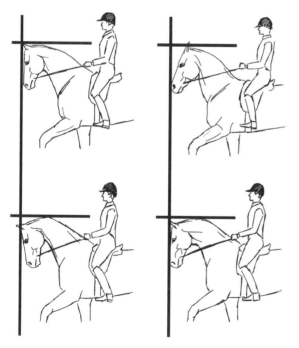

Top left – on the bit: correct. Top right – above the bit, off the aids, hollow: incorrect. Bottom left – behind the vertical, behind the bit, broken neck: incorrect. Bottom right – on the vertical but behind the bit, broken neck: incorrect.

Behind the Bit

Being 'behind the bit' can be less obviously apparent, as the horse can look to be in an 'outline' with an arched neck, and often has what seems to be a very light contact. He is behind the vertical with, in the extreme case, his chin on his chest, and often also has a 'broken' neck. (This phenomenon is clearly shown in the photograph, and is totally man, or should we say hand, made.) Such a horse is effectively unreachable and untrainable, as he is not working 'through', and is definitely not 'on the bit' or 'into the contact', so the rider has nothing with which to work – the horse is out of control! Any 'training' is going to be of the forced variety.

Telltale signs include coming ever lower, hollowing, trailing hindlegs, becoming short in the neck and tight at the poll, lacking forward energy, running away, and being very difficult to turn even in walk.

This is much more of a challenge to deal with than nearly any level of being 'above the bit'. The rider needs to push the horse carefully and steadily into a forward, following contact, being content with small steps towards the horse offering to take the contact, but not going so much forwards that the horse rushes off and the rider has to take a strong contact. Maintenance or establishment of a consistent rhythm is the first step. The aim is to get the horse to stretch his head and neck forwards towards the contact and accept it.

Since this fault is almost always the result of too strong a contact that is not backed up by driving aids, it follows that this rehabilitation is a real juggling act and best left to a rider who is able to adjust the contact and the balance without relying on his hands. Sadly a loose rein doesn't work here, as the horse then has no reason at all to work forwards to the contact, as there won't be one!

So it is back to trust, this time from the rider to the horse.

The length and tautness (not looseness or tightness) of the rein are clearly within the rider's sphere: as we said earlier, it will depend upon the physical length of the horse's frame, but also on the pace being worked in, as each pace demands a slightly different rein length to accommodate the necessary neck length (with the walk being the longest, and the canter being the shortest), and on the stage of training.

● Nothing in the training of horses is a separate issue, and success is really the ability to blend all the information into a holistic way of riding.

Snaffles: left, too high; right, too low.

Well fitted snaffle, with a drop noseband.

SPEAKING OF BRIDLES AND BITS

Make sure that the bridle fits the horse – and make even more sure that the bit is the correct size and in the correct place in the mouth, and that it's neither too thick nor too thin, as horses' mouths vary considerably in size, palate height and tongue thickness. Flash nosebands are most commonly seen in dressage, although some horses go well in a drop noseband and the Micklem bridle is gaining some support (*see* Further Information, page 172). Whatever the choice of noseband, don't winch it in so tight that the horse is in a vice just so you can 'control' him, and don't have the drop so low that the horse has trouble breathing.

If you ride in a double bridle, the fit is even more crucial as the pressures that can be brought to bear on the horse's head, nose and all aspects of his mouth are magnified by the two bits and the leverage of the curb and chain. The curb chain should fit into the chin groove and be tight enough to allow only 45 degrees of leverage when the reins are taken up. Any tighter and your horse is likely to stand on his hindlegs a lot; any looser and the curb bit rolls over in the mouth and is horizontal viewed from the side when the reins are taken up.

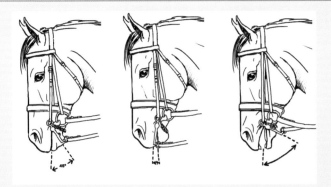

Double bridles: left, ideal angle; middle, curb chain too tight, too much poll pressure; right, curb chain too loose, bit horizontal.

- A loose curb chain isn't 'kind', it is just wrongly fitted, and totally messes up the purpose of the double bridle; furthermore with unfeeling hands at the end of the reins, it can be tantamount to abuse.

Double bridles can be seen in use in many of the photographs in this book. The doubles are well fitted, although several are not being used as they should be. It's also educational to observe the differing ways in which the two reins can be held.

Finally it is important to keep the leather clean, supple and in good repair.

You know this combination by now – a well fitted double with the horse working confidently into the bridle.

8 Transitions

Transitions are the phases between paces, and within paces, where a change of some sort is required. They are part of the half-halt process and the half-halt process is part of transitions; the two should be inseparable and indivisible.

At the most basic level, transitions are how you start and stop and get from one pace to another. At another level, they are the practical application of the Scales of Training, and enable a rider to train a horse correctly through to all the work at Grand Prix.

The concept of transitions is simple; however, the application is not always so easy. Their importance to training is underlined by the number of transitions in any dressage test, and the fact that they are, more often than not, worthy of a separate mark, or are the arbiters of the mark in a series of movements. They are the gears, and the more smoothly they are applied, the less noticeable they become, and your horse looks to be doing everything on his own! Knowledgeable riders ride many transitions in a training session, whether half-halts or actual transitions.

Transitions teach collection and develop extension; they develop the longitudinal suppleness of the horse, and increase his gymnastic ability and flexibility. They are the main means of communication between horse and rider. They are the lifeblood of riding.

THE HALT

The most basic transitions are from stop to go, and go to stop. All horses need to learn these for everyone's safety. If the horse is young or inexperienced, then the simpler the method, the better. Kyra Kyrklund's philosophy of using 'stop/start' is just that. At the beginning, using both legs on the girth means start. Using both hands on the reins, followed by an immediate give, repeated as necessary in conjunction with the rider restricting the movement in his midriff, means stop. Use your voice as well.

So the horse learns to go forwards from the leg, and to stop with the reins: simple. What is crucial is that these basic aids are obeyed, so a light tap with the whip might be necessary for the forward movement. If this isn't enough, then a 'louder' aid with a spur, or a more pronounced kick needs to be used. However, you also need to be ready for a more extreme reaction to such an aid, and allow the forward movement and go with it – then bring the horse back to a steadier pace, and then stop again.

Once this system is in place, then the lighter the aids, the better.

The above is far from sophisticated, but that's the point. When a horse starts the learning process, too many signals all at once will simply confuse and upset him; one aid, or at the most two aids, at a time are enough.

Understanding has to be developed slowly and carefully – the basis of the stop/go system.

The voice can be most useful, as the horse should know the command 'walk on' and also the noise or word you use to get him to stop moving!

Imported horses are used to hearing the noise 'brrrrr' or 'prrrrr' (preferably with a really good roll to the 'r' !): to them, this means 'stop', or at least 'stop what you're doing'. More than a few English native speakers think that it means 'go faster' – it doesn't, and this can make for some confused horses and interesting scenarios!

Initially, if the horse panics when asked to stand still, it can make things worse to insist. Walk forwards and try again, quite often, until the horse settles. This can take some time, and calm repetition is the key; don't get cross, don't panic, just carefully and slowly find a way to get rid of the horse's perception that he can't stay still in balance, which is often the underlying problem.

Other horses are quite simply impatient, so the halt needs to be just part of the overall work, introduced every so often and without tension. In such a case, it can be a good idea to do some work first to reduce the energy levels and allow for some influence on the horse's brain, before asking for any proper halts!

It can be amazingly difficult to get a horse to stop when asked – he creeps forwards step by step, or he jogs and fidgets. Take care that you're not using your seat and legs in a way that is actually asking him to continue to walk forwards at the same time as your hands are saying stop. Effectively, you need to stop moving with your body and be passive with your seat and legs so that the horse isn't confused by conflicting aids. Some horses react well to a momentary squeezing with the knees at the same time as you ask with your hands. Working on a smallish circle, or heading directly towards (not into!) the wall of the school can be most helpful here. Use your voice. Trying to stop on the 'open' side of a circle, or on the straight on the long side of an arena, just makes the task more difficult.

Be satisfied with a 'stop' that can be maintained for 'x' number of seconds – 'x' being the length of time you can get the horse to remain stationary so that you ask him to move off before he thinks of it for himself! Don't worry where each of his legs is: when 'stop' is no longer a problem, you can work on getting him to step into the rein from behind, and start to learn to halt square. Your horse should be prepared to stop, never mind halt, any time you ask him to do so.

Practising the halt from the walk teaches the horse to accept a little pressure from the bit, and to yield and slow when asked.

If the rider simply pulls back on the reins to halt, the horse will come to an abrupt stop, on the forehand, unbalanced and uncoordinated. This can also have the effect of worrying him and teaching him to fidget and/or refuse to stand still, to open his mouth, stick his head in the air, rear, and use any of the other evasions that pulling on the reins can produce.

In a test situation one often sees riders in rising trot, only apparently remembering at the last moment that they have to halt; these halts are almost always done on the hand, losing any harmony, fluency and balance that might have been possible had the halt been remembered earlier!

● Rising trot to halt is very difficult to carry off successfully.

The more refined version of the stop/go transition is that the horse learns to halt and move off 'on the aids'. The rider ceases to follow the horse's movement and sits more upright, with a very light closing of the leg in conjunction with a taking and giving rein, until the horse halts. When this is achieved, the rider gives with the reins just enough that the horse moves neither forwards nor backwards but stays comfortably 'on the aids', is stationary, and gives at the poll and jaw. The perfect square halt means that only two legs can be seen when

viewed from the front, the back or the sides. The move-off from halt should be immediate, without resistance and without lurching forwards or drifting sideways.

Halts need careful, correct, considered riding. If your horse doesn't halt or stop well from walk, it isn't likely that he will do so from trot or canter!

THE HALF-HALT

The half-halt is the tool with which you warn, prepare, bring to attention and generally organize your horse before you ask him to do something; for instance, before any exercise or movement (circle, corner, turn, lateral work) you want to ride.

Half-halts are used to balance, re-balance, improve the contact, shorten, straighten, collect, position, turn and make transitions where the half-halt specifically engages the hindlegs. They are completely indispensable and should be used often – *they are half a halt.* When asked how many half-halts he gave

TOP LEFT: A back view of halt, with only two legs visible: Laura Bechtolsheimer (GB) and Mistral Hojris.

BOTTOM LEFT: A side view of halt, with only two legs visible.

during a working session, Colonel Podhajsky (the late Director of the Spanish Riding School in Vienna) apparently said that he'd never counted, but he was sure it was in excess of 500!

Given that a horse cannot possibly know what you have planned, it does seem only fair that some warning is given before action is required – so start with a half-halt, move on to the aid, and then allow the horse to do what is asked.

- Prepare, ask, allow and reward.

You have to train half-halts; horses don't know about them automatically, and half-halts only work when the horse knows about, and reacts easily to, the aids and is 'on the bit'. The half-halt is probably the most misunderstood and misridden of all training techniques. Jumping riders 'check' or 'take a pull' to shorten the horse into or between fences – this tends to suggest that it's just the hand which does this; the better jump riders use the rein in conjunction with their seat and legs to keep the horse coming forwards but shorter in the stride. Dressage riders also often just use their hands.

How to Ride a Half-Halt

To ride a half-halt, the rider sits up a bit straighter, stretching through the sternum, puts weight into the already central seat via the seatbones, and closes the legs lightly round the horse's ribcage, thus closing the horse up from behind into a momentarily restraining hand, then gives the hand and relaxes the seat and leg. In this way, the horse is shortened, restrained and allowed in the space of, at most, three seconds, thus balancing him before whatever comes next. At no point should the rider lean back; this doesn't achieve anything other than weakening the seat and causing the horse to hollow.

Keep the half-halt short, never longer than three seconds, and repeat as necessary. Sometimes a bit more seat and leg might be necessary, but never a stronger more prolonged rein aid, whatever the provocation.

When the half-halt comes through – that is, the horse has understood the aids – this is the moment to ask/tell the horse what you want – a downward or upward transition, for which you then give the required and understood aid, or a lateral movement that requires positioning and bend. It may well be that, during the transition, further half-halts will be needed to ensure that the fluency, suppleness and balance remain intact.

- You can now see why we constantly emphasize that the rider needs good co-ordination, balance and independence of seat.

Half-halts can be likened to cycling downhill: if you apply the brakes lightly and quite often, you can control the speed, maintain balance and enjoy the speed, whilst arriving at the bottom of the hill in one piece, and still in control and balance. In the same way, driving a car on the accelerator and brakes alone, without using the clutch to change gear, is quite possible but is noisy and rough. Maintaining control with a judicious mix of gears, accelerator and brakes makes the whole experience much more enjoyable and safe. So it is with the constant use of half-halts.

WALK AND TROT TRANSITIONS

The walk before an upward transition needs to be active and with enough of a forward tendency (but not hurried or quick) so that the horse is almost thinking about it for himself and the aid is just permission for him to go. The transition will only be as good as the energy of the pace from which it is being made.

The aids are a light push with both seatbones, in conjunction with a light aid from both legs, into a rein which allows the upward movement without losing the contact – it can help to think of having ½lb (500g) in the hands. Even at the beginning of training, sitting for a couple of strides to make sure the transition has worked is a good idea, and then the rider can rise to the trot.

If the contact is too loose, the horse can easily fall on to the forehand. Conversely, too tight a rein will simply mean the horse won't go forwards into trot, and he is likely to hollow and throw his head up; effectively you're saying 'go' with your seat and leg aids, and 'stop' with your hands, which confuses and upsets him.

Coming from trot to walk, the rider should sit for a few strides before the walk so that the forward tendency isn't lost. As we've said before, rising trot to walk (or halt) is not going to achieve a fluent transition, and the horse has no way of knowing that he is expected to change pace if he's given no warning.

Sit tall through the sternum, cease the 'trot' movement with your pelvis whilst keeping your legs close to the horse's sides, and momentarily close your hands on the reins. If you need to, use your voice so that your horse gets a clear message.

The moment you feel the horse change pace from trot to walk, make sure that your hands allow the walk to come through without any loss of fluency, and begin to follow the movement of the head and neck so that your horse can walk on without tension or resistance. Don't 'give' the reins by coming forward with your arms so much that you lose the contact, because this will mean the horse will continue to trot or become unbalanced; neither should you be applying a backward aid with the reins, because this will shorten the neck and restrict the horse when what you want is for him to walk forwards.

The result of any of the above is likely to be that he learns to jog, or at least won't have the confidence to walk forwards in a relaxed way into the rein.

Trot, Walk, Trot

The transition from trot to walk then back into trot again is the next stage, and is a valuable check on your horse's understanding of the aids. It also helps with increasing the energy and engagement from behind, and encourages the horse to work with suppleness over his back to the contact.

If the horse is too abrupt into the walk and almost stops, check that you weren't over-enthusiastic with your rein aids, and don't continue in walk but go forwards into trot again; try the transition again after a few strides.

Too much restriction with the reins whilst asking the horse to trot is likely to result in the horse hollowing in his back, shortening his neck and otherwise resisting the forward aids. So you need to allow the trot by controlling the amount you give with the reins so that he can be ridden forwards into the contact.

A good way into the trot, if there is some resistance to the trot aids, is to do a few steps of leg yield in the walk as, very often, sending the horse sideways releases the block and makes him more willing to go forwards. This is most easily done in a corner or on a circle when he is often more than willing to displace his quarters, but then you need to be quick to straighten him and ask for the trot transition again. This really only works if you don't lose the bit of flexibility that the leg yield has created, so you're looking at one or two straight strides at the most.

If your horse offers canter rather than trot, it's usually because your leg aids are uneven and/or the contact is stronger on one rein than the other, or there is tension and evasion. Bring him back to trot – voice aids can be useful – and try again, with equal feel in both reins, without over-restricting him, and making sure that you give simultaneous aids with both legs so that the horse isn't confused and understands to go into trot. You can also use lateral work to good effect, either shoulder-fore or shoulder-in, to regain the trot.

TROT, CANTER, TROT TRANSITIONS

The mere fact that the horse has to rearrange his legs to go from a diagonal two-beat pace, trot, into an asymmetric three-beat pace, canter, is quite a gymnastic feat, and it's much easier for him to do this if he isn't tight over his back.

The rider needs to change the position of his seat in the saddle from the 'trot seat', where he sits on both seatbones equally, and both legs are in a similar position, into the 'canter seat' where the inner seatbone is more weighted and the inside hip is forward, the outside leg is back from the hip behind the girth, and the inside leg is at the girth. For these aids to be successful, the rider should sit to the trot.

The rider needs to have a consistent, quiet contact that allows the horse to draw forwards into the canter without giving the reins so much that the horse just trots faster or runs through the reins into canter. Preparation is crucial, so the rider's outside leg going back is the first indication to the horse that something is coming; in conjunction with a half-halt on the outside rein and some inside flexion from the inside rein, the inside leg then gives an active aid and this is when the horse should go into canter.

However, before the active aid to canter is given, the horse should accept the outside leg being back and should not take this as the aid to canter. He should continue to trot, accept the half-halt by staying soft at the poll and jaw, and then the active inside leg aid to canter can be given. For these aids to be successful, the rider should sit in the trot.

The reasons for this deliberate preparation are so that the horse learns to wait without tension for the active aid, and also learns that canter is

Through the corner – a good place to ask for a canter transition.

initiated by the rider's inside leg. This acceptance of the passive outside leg being back behind the girth is something that, later on, becomes very useful as it should be less confusing for the horse when riding trot half-pass, where the rider positions his outside leg similarly but doesn't want canter.

Given that riders and horses can find canter worrying, this sort of preparation is a good mental exercise. The rider needs to ensure that his outside leg is back in the canter position, with a lowered heel, without becoming tight in the knee or gripping the horse's side; it should be passive and comfortable. Riders and horses should keep breathing and stay relaxed!

A canter transition is most easily ridden on a bent line – through a corner or on a circle or loop – because the horse is more inclined to stay engaged, and the inside hindleg is more likely to be under the centre of gravity.

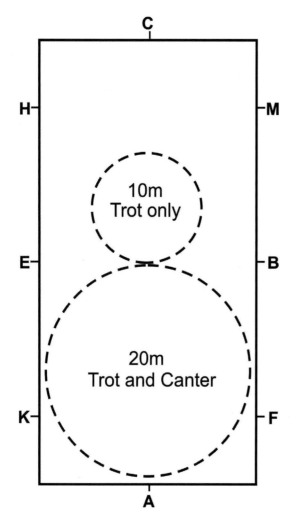

Trot/canter/trot exercise on two circles.

side of the arena if your horse is inclined to rush off – that is, give the aids to canter when the horse is turned towards the short side of the arena or towards the wall, rather than on the 'open' side where there is nothing to back him off; stay on a circle or return to a circle line rather than use straight lines; use smaller circles (but not so small that the horse is unbalanced) to make downward transitions, and again, avoid the 'open' side of the arena where the horse can see a long straight line ahead

Of course, if your horse is backward thinking, initiating the canter coming out of a corner on to the 'open' arena could be exactly what's needed to encourage him to think forwards.

One good exercise to improve left and right strike-offs into canter is to ride a 20m circle in trot at A or C (in the small arena) and over X, change the rein on to a 10m circle still in trot; as you approach X again, you're going to change the rein and also ask for canter at the same time and ride canter on the 20m circle.

On returning to X, make a transition from canter to trot and change the rein in trot on to a 20m circle, at X again ride another change of rein on to a 10m circle, still in trot. On returning to X, change the rein, ask for canter, on to a 20m circle. And so on. Make sure you keep the size and shape of the circles. The 10m trot circles are best done in sitting trot but you need to keep the forwardness of the trot so that there's enough energy for your horse to pop into canter.

Transitions need to be as well ridden as they can be so that the horse learns to make good ones – try to ask for them at opportune moments and not when he's unbalanced, bearing down on the bit, sticking his nose in the air, or busy spooking at something in the hedge!

The smoothness of transitions is more important in the early stages than where exactly the transition is made, as the latter puts too much pressure on rider and horse. When the actual canter transition is no longer an issue, then more accuracy can be introduced.

If, after all this, you find you struggle to make transitions where you'd like to, there are a couple of things to try. Use the arena to help you; as we've said already, it is generally easier to pick up canter in a corner or on a circle than on a straight line. Use the 'closed'

● Remember, bad habits are just as easy to learn as good ones, and they seem to be the ones that persist!

9 Straightness

Ask me to show you poetry in motion and I will show you a horse.

(Unknown)

Although straightness is not first in the Scales of Training, there are strong arguments for paying attention to the innate crookedness of the horse early in training because straightness is a fundamental requirement of 'throughness' (*Durchlässigkeit*) – you bend your horse to straighten him. If you think about it, it's not likely that the horse's full power can be developed if one of his hindlegs is displaced to the side and isn't taking equal weight, because he won't be in balance.

It is really important to understand, and acknowledge, that this matter of straightness ideally needs consideration from the moment a horse starts ridden work.

The FEI definition of 'straight' is:

> Equal bend in both reins. The horse is straight when the forehand is in line with the hindquarters; that is, when the longitudinal axis is in line with the straight or curved track it is following.

Since one of the basic tenets of training is that the horse needs to be straight, this is something that the rider needs to recognize and address. The aim is to have the head and neck straight in front of you, and if on a curved line, not showing more bend in the neck than in the body, with an even feel into both reins, and the ability to flex equally to the left and to the right. The horse should track into, or over, the print of the front feet with the back ones, apart from in collected work. Also, the rider's legs should be able to hang down on each side of the horse comfortably in the correct position, with no unequal push of the ribcage against either leg.

Straight in walk: the hind feet stepping into the tracks of the fore feet – left hind, left fore, right hind, right fore.

● You could say that 'straight' means equal – equal into both reins, equal weight over all four legs, equal power coming from both hindlegs, equal facility to bend both ways.

BEND

Bend is the curve of the horse's body round the rider's inside leg through corners and on bent lines, and should correspond to the ground pattern of the movement being performed – so the bend needed for a 20m circle is quite slight, whereas for an 8m volte it's more obvious.

The neck from poll to withers is the most 'bendy' part of the horse's body. The shoulders are not attached to the skeleton by bone; they sit in a sling, which allows each shoulder quite a bit of individual freedom of movement – so the horse is able to 'bend' somewhat to the action of the rider's inside leg, in conjunction with a bend in the neck, in spite of the fact that the back and ribcage are the most rigid parts of the structure with very little actual movement.

TOP LEFT: Bent through the corner in canter.

BOTTOM LEFT: Bent through the corner in trot.

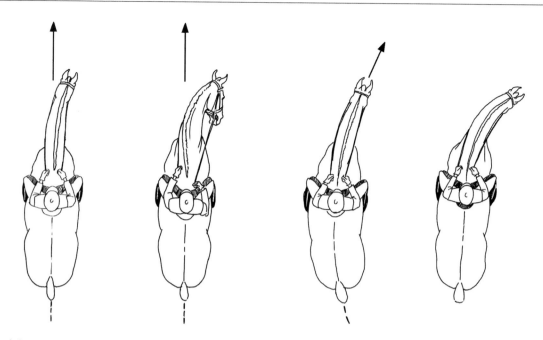

Far left: correct position on a straight line, with slight flexion to the inside; second left: too much neck bend on a straight line; right: correct flexion on a curved line; far right too much neck bend on curved line.

Stimulation via the rider's leg on one side of the ribcage creates a slight 'give' away from the pressure, which is visible on the other side of the horse as a slight bulge – so concave on one side and convex on the other, by courtesy of the muscles contracting on one side and expanding on the other. However, this only works if the rider's outside leg stops the horse from swinging his quarters out, away from the action of the inside leg.

So we are, in fact, talking about an illusion of bend from the withers back, and the gymnastic ability of the horse to perform movements requiring 'bend' has to be built up progressively. Essentially bend comes from the neck and the 'give' in the ribcage.

In Harry Boldt's famous book *Das Dressurpferd* (*see* Further Information, page 172), there are many photographs taken from above of circles and lateral work, and these show conclusively that bend is really only demonstrated in the neck. The back from the withers to the tail is virtually straight: there is a very slight tilt of the hips to the inside, the hindlegs are engaged and are under the centre of gravity with no displacement left or right, the horse is upright to the outside rein, and his balance is outstanding – and as a result of all this, he looks bent through his body!

FLEXION

Flexion is commonly used in reference to the poll – the top of the neck just behind the ears – and the relaxation of the jaw. Precisely, it occurs between the hinged joint (atlanto-occipital) where the skull meets the first cervical vertebra (atlas). Flexion can be longitudinal and lateral: the former denotes 'giving' at the poll, the latter means the horse can articulate left or right at the poll. Bend uses the whole neck; flexion is confined to the poll, but is necessary for successful bending.

In order to successfully flex the horse left or right, the poll and jaw must first be relaxed enough to allow this – they must be without tension or resistance – and the head must be vertical. What happens then, when you flex, is that the muscles under the crest of the mane can 'flip' from one side to the other, very clearly, without a bend in the neck. A horse that's tight in the poll and jaw, or sticks his head up or out, away from the vertical, can't show this reaction as the joint becomes locked and lateral flexion is not possible (and head tilting is one visible outcome).

When you turn your head to look where you're going, your body follows and there's very little tension in your neck and no excessive movement is necessary. If you try to turn whilst keeping your head and neck away from the turn, tension inevitably creeps in and you make it difficult for yourself. (*See* Chapter 4, page 27, for more on 'flexing at the poll' as a rider.) So, articulating at the poll means that the horse can flex left or right towards the direction in which he is going whilst keeping everything in alignment. This is important for keeping his balance and straightness through turns and circles.

CROOKEDNESS

We are all aware that most people are right-handed – that is, they favour their right hand and right-hand side over their left – and the others are left-handed (and some people are ambidextrous, but there are always exceptions!). Horses also have a 'right-handed' tendency, with a similar majority – they favour, and put more weight on, the right front leg and the right hindleg, while other horses have a 'left-handed' tendency. These tendencies are more or less pronounced in each individual person and equine.

● Natural straightness and symmetry in either species – horses or people – are both so rare as to be negligible.

Anatomically the horse is wider behind than in front – he is triangular in shape – so the rider should always aim to straighten the horse via the shoulders rather than the hindquarters: in other words, align the shoulders to the hindquarters. This anatomical fact also means that if you have the horse's head, neck and shoulders too close to the wall of the school he will, of necessity, have his quarters to the inside – he'll be crooked – and this is particularly the case in canter.

When you get on a horse, you need to discover whether he is left- or right-'handed'. On taking the reins up, there will be more 'feel', more weight, in one rein than in the other, so this is the rein the horse favours. For instance, on the left rein the horse is heavier in the left hand and lighter on the right and has an inclination to want to look to the right (keeping his own bend to the right), and this

Hips wider than the shoulders.

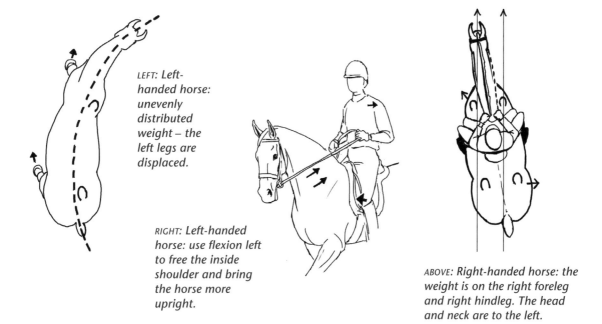

LEFT: *Left-handed horse: unevenly distributed weight – the left legs are displaced.*

RIGHT: *Left-handed horse: use flexion left to free the inside shoulder and bring the horse more upright.*

ABOVE: *Right-handed horse: the weight is on the right foreleg and right hindleg. The head and neck are to the left.*

doesn't alter when you change the rein from left to right.

How to Correct Crookedness

A left-handed horse will put his weight excessively on to the left foreleg and left hindleg. This restricts the action of the left (inside) hindleg and takes the weight off the right hindleg, and the head and neck are carried to the right, as illustrated in the drawing above – it is somewhat exaggerated to make the point!

By flexing the neck to the left, the left shoulder draws back and the weight can transfer from the left shoulder diagonally to the right hindleg, which now becomes the weight-carrying, supporting leg. When this has happened, the horse's inside (left) hindleg is free to step forwards under the centre of gravity and support the left hindquarters, which also has the effect of lightening the left shoulder – and your horse will become more upright and straighter.

However, horses – and in fact all mammals – have what is called 'muscle memory'. This means that the horse returns to what his body naturally wants to do, and thus straightening exercises are, effectively, ongoing; over time, however, the new muscle memory does start to take precedence.

To achieve this correction in the left-handed horse, the rider puts his weight on the left seatbone, with the knee slightly closed into the horse's left shoulder, and the heel deep (without leaning over or losing the central, balanced position). The left hand is slightly raised, and the shoulder drawn back as left neck bend is asked for: this has the effect that the horse should come more underneath the rider's right seatbone as the horse takes more weight on to that right hindleg. The ribcage should curve slightly to the right and will, therefore, come more into contact with the rider's right leg. This, in turn, should mean that the rider feels more supported under both seatbones and is sitting square on a more level back.

On changing the rein from left to right, the horse needs to remain in left flexion (counter

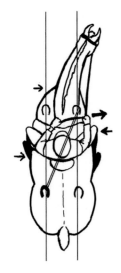

BELOW: *Straight horse.*

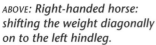

ABOVE: *Right-handed horse: shifting the weight diagonally on to the left hindleg.*

flexion) because otherwise he will step to the outside with his left hindleg, and you're back where you started.

To summarize, the left-handed horse needs to be ridden in left bend on the left rein and also left bend on the right rein (counter flexion), until he has developed more equally on both reins and remains more often upright and straight. All the above is reversed for a right-handed horse.

SUMMARY

Thus far we've talked about straightening by bending and/or flexing. Ultimately you want a straight horse equal in both reins, and throughout the work you test for straightness and balance by giving forwards with one and/or both reins, and also, fairly obviously, by not bending or flexing at all, and seeing what transpires.

Riders who sit to one side, whether because the horse 'puts' them there or because they are not conscious of sitting crookedly in the saddle,

make it very difficult for the horse to deal with the shifted weight, and he necessarily finds himself out of balance. In addition, the horse is likely to become sore in his back on one side and to develop the musculature unevenly. All this adds an unwanted dimension to the issues of straightness in the horse.

- Once more for emphasis: correct training is difficult to achieve without the ability to flex and bend the horse, and it is this that renders the horse supple, straight and energetic.

Like all corrective exercises, straightening the horse takes considerable time, repetition and patience. However, the end result is a straighter horse with the full power and energy of the hindquarters available to be released, and with the flexibility to bend and flex equally left and right, without any deviation of the hindquarters, and with equal weight over all four legs.

It is important that riders recognize and address their core stability and that of their horses (*see* Chapters 4 and 5). When the horse is straight, conditioning his core musculature is easier to achieve as part of the process of turning him into the athlete he should be. There are some exercises that can be introduced from the ground to help the horse's mobility and core strength, such as tempting the horse to turn his head and neck as far as possible in order to get at the carrot you're holding, without moving his legs or falling over. Quite a few of the exercises sound simple but require some practice and expertise, and therefore we feel that including explanations and diagrams is beyond the scope of this book.

This is an extensive subject in its own right. It is covered in detail in Dr H. M. Clayton and Dr N. C. Stubbs' book, *Activate Your Horse's Core.* Exercises for the rider are many and various, but we have found those in Dr Eckart Meyner's DVD *Movement Awareness for Riders* to be very helpful.

10 Impulsion and Collection

In riding a horse, we borrow freedom.

(Helen Thompson)

Impulsion – controlled energy, or 'dynamic energy' as Betsy Steiner calls it – is really only properly released when the horse is straight. This makes some sense, as it must be virtually impossible to deliver true thrust forwards from the hindlegs if they aren't aligned behind the front legs – the power is perhaps not totally lost, but must be lessened if one of the hindlegs is out to the side somewhere. The spring, bounce, the cadence of impulsion means the horse is bending all the joints of both hindlegs and using his back to transmit the created energy to the contact, which must be hard to do when one hindleg is displaced.

Horses have 'rear engine drive'. Impulsion is not about speed. Balance, relaxation, straightness and energy are the gears. There is nothing hurried about a horse with impulsion:

Impulsion in action in trot.

Impulsion in action in canter.

he looks more expressive and impressive, and his paces are not flat and earthbound but full of spring, vitality and cadence. The horse takes weight behind, is equal into both reins, and is straight.

Cadence in trot and canter can be difficult to interpret, but may be expressed as the culmination of controlled energy and impulsion, engagement from behind, swing and spring off the ground – the moment of suspension – together with metronomic regularity and rhythm. The steps should be equally proportioned, with the same length behind and in front, and in trot, with cannon bones parallel with each other. A horse with an exaggerated, dramatic action of the forelimbs can look amazing, but unless such action is mirrored

with the hindlegs, it is not correct, and is often accompanied by some hollowing over the back (the former are back movers, the latter are leg movers).

There are some horses, of course, that have a predisposition towards this sort of leg movement – Hackneys, Gelderlanders, Welsh Cobs, for instance – but this can't always be assumed to be impulsion (unless it is, of course!).

Some horses have more natural energy than others, but the extra surge of energy that can be released when the horse is straight and balanced is amazing, and horses that have previously been described as 'lazy' are often galvanized into action – which can't be bad. Impulsion is something that can be taught to most horses that are correctly trained; natural energy is great, but acquired energy can be developed.

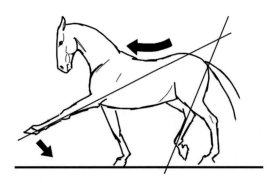

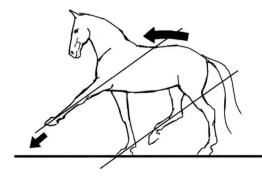

Leg mover: hollow back, tight neck, the foreleg action more exaggerated than the hindleg action and not matched in height and reach. Back mover: working over the back with good topline definition, the angles in front and behind matching, and the power free to flow through the body.

IMPULSION IN THE PACES

Walk has energy and activity but no impulsion or cadence as there is always one foot on the ground, thus there is no moment of suspension. Trot and canter should be full of impulsion, and very collected work in either pace can demonstrate enormous power and impulsion, although it's probably true to say that the energy is more obviously dynamic in the extended paces.

The FEI gives the following definition of impulsion:

Thrust. Releasing the energy stored by engagement. In dressage, impulsion is associated with a phase of suspension such as exists in trot and canter, but which does not exist in walk. Therefore, impulsion is not applicable in walk.

British Dressage has this to say about impulsion:

> Impulsion is the term used to describe the transmission of an eager and energetic, yet controlled, propulsive energy generated from the hindquarters into the athletic movement of the horse. Its ultimate expression can be shown only through the horse's soft and swinging back to be guided by a gentle contact with the rider's hand.
>
> …Speed, of itself, has little to do with impulsion; the result (of speed) is more often a flattening of the paces. A visible characteristic is a more pronounced articulation of the hindleg, in a continuous rather than staccato action. The hock, as the hind foot leaves the ground, should first move forwards rather than being pulled upwards, but certainly not backwards. A prime ingredient of impulsion is the time the horse spends in the air rather than on the ground; in other words, an added expression within the paces, always provided that there is a clear distinction between the collected trot and the Passage. Impulsion is, therefore, only seen in those paces that have a period of suspension.

The Germans have one word that encapsulates all the above: *Schwung*. It means swing, plus elasticity and suppleness over the back, cadence, spring and power, which adds considerably more complexity than our word 'swing' suggests on its own.

DEVELOPING THE ENERGY

At first, sending the horse actively forwards will develop the pushing power of the hindquarters.

Pushing is what the horse does when he is activated by the rider's seat and legs to place his hindlegs more underneath his centre of gravity. This is most easily seen by watching the placement of the inside hindleg when he steps forwards with it, taking the weight and propelling himself forwards into the next stride.

Horses naturally carry more of their own weight over their forelimbs; when we ride them we make this imbalance between front and rear even more pronounced. One of the fundamental aims of training is to find a way to redress this balance so that the horse carries more weight over the hindlegs, so that riding is safer and easier for both parties.

The 'give and retake' of the reins when schooling, or in a test, is one way of checking how the horse's self-carriage is progressing. (*See* Chapter 13 for more on 'give and retake'.)

Through consistent use of half-halts and transitions within the paces, to and from and up and down the paces, plus lateral work, the carrying power of the hindlegs is developed (together with the pushing) so that the horse learns to work with suppleness over the back from behind to the contact to create enough impulsion for true self-carriage. However, it is important that the core muscles and the abdominal muscles of the horse are involved in this process; it is the 'recruitment' of the abdominal muscles that lifts the back and supports it, which in turn allows the power from the hindlegs to come through. (*See* 'Core Stability' at the end of Chapter 4.)

Without impulsion true collection cannot exist. In collection the steps become shorter, often undertracking, but are active and energetic to show a clear uphill tendency. Wolfgang Niggli, in his book *Dressage – a Guideline for Riders and Judges*, explains collection quite clearly:

> … Through correct training, the horse develops in his hindquarters the power to carry his body and the weight of his rider (vertical lifting power), as well as the power to move forwards (horizontal pushing).

Niggli goes on to say that, in collection, the two components are approximately the same, so the forces created equalize and the horse comes into collection. The *Concise Oxford English*

Vertical lifting power increased, horizontal pushing power reduced.

Dictionary gives the following definition of 'collect', which sums it up rather well: 'Bring or gather together; systematically seek and acquire.'

Without impulsion and collection, correct extension can't exist. As Niggli explains, when one of the components is increased or reduced, the horse's frame and length of stride will alter accordingly. So, for example, if the horizontal pushing power is increased and the vertical lifting power is reduced, the horse will go into medium trot. If the horizontal power is used to the maximum, an extended trot (or canter) will result.

For passage and piaffe, the vertical lifting power would need to be increased and the horizontal pushing power reduced accordingly, so that the horse could take weight behind, lift and lighten the forehand, and shorten the strides into a cadenced, elevated movement.

You could say that the first three Scales of Training – rhythm, suppleness and contact – are good and essential building blocks for any well trained horse in whatever discipline. They are certainly necessary for straightness, and this, in turn, is necessary for impulsion and collection. Taken to the ultimate, these latter two qualities are more or less the exclusive territory of the advanced dressage horse. Correctly applied, the combination of all the Scales, but particularly the second trio, means that the horse learns to bend the joints in the hindlegs equally so that he can 'sit' or lower the croup at the same time as the shoulders are freed. In this way, the life and expression in the paces are developed.

The optical illusion this creates is that the forehand seems to be higher – although in fact it can't be, other than that the horse comes up a bit in the withers: the forelegs are the length they are, and can't magically 'come up'!

The total acceptance by the horse of the half-halt is indispensable as, without this, there is always going to be a training issue with both impulsion and collection. The controlled energy needs to be readily available, to be released in smaller or larger doses according to the work for which the rider asks – and that is what acceptance of the bit and the aids are all about.

In all this, it mustn't be forgotten that the neck will be shorter and more raised in collection than in extension. The poll should remain the highest point with the nose very slightly in front of the vertical in collection, and rather more so in extension. Over-shortening with the reins only creates a tense, hollow horse and has no place when discussing impulsion and collection. In extension, the frame should be extended forwards so that the horse can release his power: done well, just that slight lengthening of the frame really 'allows' the extension. If the only way to achieve an extension is to lean back, shove with your body and kick like the devil, there is something badly amiss with the training and the resulting extension is unlikely to be rhythmic, balanced and equal in front and behind!

Collection is the culmination of the correct application of the Scales of Training, and tremendous feel and empathy between horse and rider. It is not something that can be forced on to the horse: the strength in the back, the core muscles, the abdominal muscles and the limbs take time to be developed, and any shortcuts become apparent in a loss of power, energy and beauty.

11 Lengthening

…and I whispered to the horse: trust no man in whose eye you don't see yourself reflected as an equal.

Don Vincenzo Giobbe (c. 1700)

[Lengthening is…] elongation of the stride and the outline of the horse, yet maintaining the same tempo and balance as in the corresponding working pace.

(FEI)

Any degree of extension is only as good as the degree of collection. Think of a big, thick spring: if you simply hold it in your hand without any compression, it will just fall to the ground when you open your hand. A moderate degree of compression is necessary so that the spring can open and travel a modest distance. For extreme travel, however, you need to compress the spring strongly between your two hands and then let it go, and then it will do

what it's supposed to do, and spring! So it is with the extended paces: the horse has to

ABOVE: *Springs: no compression; moderate compression; extreme compression. Compression is needed for collection and extension.*

LEFT: *Impulsive power in trot.*

Impulsive power in canter.

understand the concept of shorter and longer strides, which is the beginning of collection.

Some horses have a natural propensity for collection, others for extension, and both extremes can be helped by training. Maximizing a horse's natural talent and minimizing his weaknesses are definitely part of the training process.

THE WALK

The FEI and British Dressage definitions of medium and extended walk are very clear:

Medium walk: A clear, regular and unconstrained walk of moderate lengthening. The horse, remaining on the bit, walks energetically but relaxed, with even and determined steps, the hind feet touching the ground in front of the hoof prints of the fore feet. The rider maintains a light, soft and steady contact with the mouth, allowing the natural movement of the head and neck.

Extended walk: The horse covers as much ground as possible, without haste and without losing the regularity of the steps. The hind feet touch the ground clearly in front of the prints of the fore feet. The rider allows the horse to stretch out the head and neck without losing contact with the mouth and control of the poll.

Free walk on a long rein has the same requirements as extended walk but with a more forwards/downwards stretch to a very light contact, to give the horse complete freedom to demonstrate an unconstrained walk with maximum purpose and long steps with a good overtrack. Note that free walk is done on a long rein, not a loose rein: there is a difference.

In the extended walk, the horse is expected to stay in a 'light and steady' contact. The steps should be as long as possible without the horse losing balance; the horse should want to stretch over his back to the rein without coming on to the forehand; equally he should come back into medium or collected walk, and thus into a more definite contact, without any resistance, change in rhythm, or slowing down of the tempo.

The collected walk is more elevated in the step, and either just tracks up or even undertracks. It is not slower in tempo nor should the activity decrease.

The walk is a marching pace: it needs to have purpose and look as though it's going somewhere without haste; each step from each leg should be of equal length; each stride has four beats to it, with an equal interval between each beat.

What often happens is that the medium walk is ridden out to the extent that there is no more overtrack or purpose that can be demonstrated in the free walk or the extended walk. Here, a bit of showmanship is necessary to demonstrate to the judge that you do know that there should be marked differences between the walks, and that you intend to show them. In any event, shortening and lengthening of the frame and the steps are part of the overall training.

Impulsion is not present in the walk as there is no moment of suspension; rather, people talk about activity and energy. However – and this is quite a big 'however' – it's easy to spoil the walk, so it is better interspersed with work in other paces to make sure the forward energy is maintained. So many people equate collection with slowness, and cause tension in their horses

in the process, as above. Lateral work can be most useful for a horse with a difficult walk as it breaks up the tracking which, in turn, reinstates the correct walk sequence, done properly.

Bear in mind that horses need to use their heads and necks to balance themselves in walk and this movement does need to be allowed, to a greater or lesser extent, in the different walks. If you set your hands and refuse to allow this movement, you will definitely cause resistance and tension in your horse's body (and mind!) as well as disturbing the purity of the walk.

Very often, 'less' is 'more' with walk, and following the rhythm of the walk with your body, or slightly resisting it, depending on what you want, whilst keeping your hands quiet, is enough to regulate the walk without nagging continually with your legs.

When giving a horse a 'rest' in walk between work sessions, free walk on a long rein is good – but this shouldn't mean that he is allowed to flop along, barely moving; the rider should keep his attention focused on the horse and make sure that the steps are long, swinging and purposeful.

If you really think the horse is too tired, then stop the work and put him away. Otherwise, bear in mind that he will have ample time for rest and relaxation when he's back in his stable or field – and he'll be there for most of the next twenty-four hours, so when he's working, make sure he also stays focused.

Note that many accidents happen at the end of work when the horse is allowed to walk as he chooses on a loose rein: if he suddenly sees or hears something that frightens him, or he stumbles, you could risk ending up on the ground.

THE TROT AND CANTER

The FEI gives the following definitions for the medium and extended paces in trot and canter:

RIGHT: **Medium trot.**

BELOW: **Extended trot: Edward Gal (Netherlands) and Moorlands Totilas.**

Medium trot: A trot with more lengthening and ground-covering steps than collected or working trot, with increased lengthening of the frame.

Extended trot: To show the utmost of impulsion in the trot strides with as much lengthening and ground cover as possible without a loss of balance.

Medium canter: An unconstrained canter with moderately extended, cadenced strides and more lengthening of the frame than at collected or working canter, while maintaining balance and an uphill tendency.

Extended canter: To demonstrate the utmost of impulsion in the canter with the cadenced strides lengthening and covering ground as much as possible without losing balance and the 'uphill' tendency.

Most riders start the trot work in the warm-up in rising trot; this applies across the board from Novice to Grand Prix. While the horse's and rider's muscles are warming up, rising trot relieves the horse of the pressure of the rider's seat on his back at every other stride and thus encourages him to become loose, relaxed and supple. This phase generally goes together with work on a long rein, on a contact, to lengthen the frame so the horse can stretch forwards/downwards.

In competition, up to and including Elementary (in the UK), rising trot is allowed in all the trot work. It is particularly useful in the lengthened paces to free the back and allow the horse to lengthen his steps without constraint from the rider (we will avoid the more esoteric argument of whether or not it's a good decision to allow rising trot at this level!).

Medium canter.

Extended canter: Imke Schellekens-Bartels (Netherlands) and Sunrise.

Changing the Diagonal

The rider should sit when the horse's inside hindleg and outside foreleg are on the ground so that his seat and leg can influence the next step that hindleg takes. Changing the diagonal regularly also exercises the muscles equally on both sides of the horse – and this should be automatic in the arena when changing the rein (sit for one extra 'bump', or three, and then rise again, checking that you are on the correct diagonal). Out hacking, try changing the diagonal every other lamp post, or every other big tree, or similar, so that this is not neglected just because you're not in an arena.

When you lengthen the strides or show medium trot on a diagonal line and you are using rising trot for all the trot work, you also need to decide when to change your own diagonal: after the corner and before your transition at the start, in the middle over X, or just before the transition at the end. Andrea goes for the first option, as you will be straightening your horse before the extension and/or setting up a slight shoulder-fore position, and this way your new inside bend is already there. The second option doesn't really work as it is difficult to do in the middle of an extension, and will be likely to unbalance both horse and rider. The third option is fine, and this is Angela's preference, except that at the end of the diagonal you already have a transition and an imminent corner, requiring a new bend and maintenance of the balance, as well as changing your own diagonal. Your choice!

If no lengthening is required and you are simply changing the rein, change your diagonal when you like but make sure you don't disturb the rhythm of the trot in the process; this is particularly the case when riding serpentine loops.

Lengthening the Frame/ Lengthening in Trot

Lengthening the frame to show 'a few lengthened strides' or 'some medium strides', applies equally to trot and canter. This lengthening is the forerunner of a full extension, and, as with most things in training, it's a progressive process. So medium strides at Novice level should show the promise of what the medium and extended extensions will finally be.

Lengthening is exactly that, and is done from a working trot (or canter); the horse needs to be going sufficiently forwards and be responsive to half-halts so that he has enough energy to increase the thrust from behind. It's not supposed to be a full extension, and at the lower levels this is not likely to come off well. The rhythm should stay the same and the tempo (speed) shouldn't get faster – the point is to produce bigger, longer strides without the horse falling on the forehand, going wide behind, becoming crooked, or losing balance.

Going wide behind is usually the result of the horse being over-pushed on to the forehand, or in a restricted frame and/or hollow, so the hindlegs have to step wide as there is not enough room for them to follow in the tracks of the forelegs. It is very difficult for a horse to lengthen his steps correctly if his frame is over-restricted.

This is often seen in conjunction with a rider leaning back behind the vertical in an attempt to 'push' the horse forwards, which keeps the rider behind the movement and causes the horse to be unable to step forwards underneath himself correctly. The result of this is that he hollows away from the extra pressure on his back, and as a result, often goes wide behind (being hollow equals lack of engagement) and, at the same time, leans on the rider's hands to keep his balance. At this point no amount of half-halting or hauling on the reins is going to alter things. It is certainly true that some horses can look spectacular from the front, but from the side or from behind they either don't cover enough ground forwards with the hindlegs, or they go wide. Once this way of going is established, it is really difficult to change it and you can see it at all levels – and it is never correct.

The rider needs to sit in a balanced, central position, with a very slight tendency forwards, so that he can follow the horse's movement with his body and his hands, and stay 'with' him, so that the horse is free to lengthen through his whole body and not just use the front legs. On its own, riding the horse strongly forwards doesn't achieve lengthening, and in fact this often puts the horse on the forehand, flattens the trot and pushes the horse out of his natural rhythm and balance, and in the process any suspension, or spring, is lost.

In order to obtain a lengthening of the frame with associated longer steps, the horse needs to be willing to stretch forwards to the contact, with a relaxed neck and a loose, swinging back – basic requirements that should be achieved in the warm-up. In this regard, there is no appreciable difference between a novice and an advanced horse.

Again and again, the rider needs to be able to make the whole frame shorter and longer at will, without the horse running away, with a corresponding shortening (into half-steps if the horse knows about them) and lengthening of the steps (on and back), so that he learns to stay in balance and begins the process of developing self-carriage. With an older, more advanced horse, the rider can think of a few steps towards piaffe when shortening the horse.

Mental relaxation is critical to these exercises as any tension will cause the horse to tighten over the back and lose the swing that gives expression to lengthening and shortening.

Shoulder-in is a very useful exercise as a way into lengthening, as the inside hindleg is already engaged. Ride through a corner into shoulder-in, say F-P, then instead of straightening on to the long side, keep the bend and lengthen across the diagonal P-S. This should also ensure that you don't turn on to the diagonal with just the inside rein which would simply make the horse crooked (something difficult to correct once on the diagonal): the horse needs to be on both reins and between both of the rider's legs (which he should be because of the shoulder-in) and thus should be able to push off both hindlegs into a powerful lengthening. Shortening again before you reach the track, go into shoulder-in S-H which completes this exercise and readjusts any loss of balance.

In order to achieve any form of lengthening, the horse has to be 'on the aids'. It is really important that he has learnt to step underneath his own centre of gravity with the inside leg, and that he is straight and can push off with both hindlegs, releasing the energy as he does so; it is also just as important that he is up to the rein – 'on the bit' – and that his nose is on, or very slightly in front of, the vertical. From this position the rider can extend the frame slightly without losing the contact and 'throughness', so that the horse can cover ground without coming on to the forehand. The rider should only attempt to lengthen the steps as much as the horse can stay in balance.

Through the use of many transitions to and from, and within the pace, the horse gradually learns to lengthen and shorten without

resistance, and this is the platform from which true extensions can be built. He must learn to 'push off the bit' (Abstossen): this is the German term and it means that the horse makes a contact which is 'feelable' in terms of weight in the hand so he is truly taking the bit, and then he yields. Sometimes this can get too strong and heavy (from the horse), but this is still better than no contact; as long as the rider feels the moment of the horse's giving to the hand and immediately yields the hand, the horse will come into a better balance and a lighter but 'there' contact. (The horse accepts the taken rein and softens to it; as he does so the rider also softens; the horse obeys the aids on the rider's softened contact.)

A useful exercise to lengthen and shorten the trot strides is to go on to a 20m circle in sitting trot. Ask for medium trot for half the circle and then, by using your core muscles and half-halts, bring him back into a more energetic, less long-striding trot, higher and rounder in the step; then repeat – on and back – so that he learns to be quick in the hindleg to respond to the lengthening and shortening aids.

When the aids are fully understood, repeat the exercise on the long side of the arena and across the diagonal lines. Rather than going all out for a long burst, which simply sends the horse on to the forehand as he loses his balance, come out of the corner and ride, say, four to eight strides of lengthening, then a similar number of shortened strides, and repeat. Use the markers to make your transitions into and out of the lengthened strides.

In a powerful medium or extended trot it's really important that the rider's body is inclined very slightly forwards in the rhythm of the pace so that he is not 'playing catch-up' with the horse's forward momentum. What is disastrous is when the rider leans back well behind the vertical, thus putting himself off balance by placing his weight too far back over the horse's loins (the weakest part of the back) at just the moment when the horse needs that area to be

Extension: Adelinde Corniellsen (Netherlands) and Parcival.

lightened so that the thrust of the hindlegs is not disturbed.

Lengthening and Shortening in Canter

Lengthening and shortening the canter is more of a challenge to the horse's balance than work in trot. As long as the horse keeps stretching to the contact and doesn't come on to the forehand, it can be most useful to put the horse into a lower outline so his back stays rounded and he can cope. The main problems that an inexperienced horse faces are a lack of strength and balance, and the canter is the pace in which strength plays a big part; it is the most

tiring phase for a horse, and too much continued work will mitigate against improvement.

Work on the circle, is good but very tiring for the horse. Using different sized circles, say from 12m to 20m, whilst shortening and lengthening the frame and the steps, works well. Giving the horse enough breaks during this work is very important.

The markers can be used to great advantage in an exercise where the lengthening is done, say, between F and B; shortening between B and M, riding with half-halts through the short side, and then shortening between H and E, and lengthening between E and K (in either arena). You can add a further dimension by counting the strides between each marker and challenging yourself to increase, or decrease, the number of strides.

It can be most useful for the rider to ride with a light seat – with the body slightly forwards and the seat out of the saddle – to relieve the pressure on the horse's back and to make sure that he is travelling in the same direction as the horse – forwards – and not hindering the horse by taking up a 'backward' position.

If you want the sort of lengthening of the stride (extension) demonstrated in the first photograph (*see* opposite), you have to work towards the compression (collection) shown in the second one – no extension without collection. Remember the springs at the beginning of the chapter!

WALKING A TIGHTROPE

Whenever new work is introduced, the temptation can be to keep on going until the horse has 'got it'. However, there's a tightrope to walk here: yes, you want to teach the horse something new and there may be some 'stressy' moments, but you don't want to sour him and make him think that learning new things always equals stress and misery.

Reward progress, however slight; give the horse frequent rests, and also intersperse new work with established work that he knows well. The benefit of this approach is that, very often, the established work improves because the stress factor goes down, and then on returning to the new lessons, both horse and rider are refreshed mentally and physically.

Collection: Steffen Peters (USA) and Ravel (piaffe).

12 Lateral Work and Pirouettes

Bread may feed my body but my horse feeds my soul.

(Unknown)

INTRODUCTION

Lateral movements are used to gymnasticize your horse on the way to collection and the more difficult movements of dressage. The movements are complete in themselves, particularly in the dressage arena, but should perhaps be better viewed as an invaluable set of tools in your 'toolbox'.

Right half-pass.

Horses do their basic work on one track. This means that the hind feet track into (or over) the prints of the front feet, when the horse is correctly positioned and ridden (this is also known as the horse being 'straight'). Lateral work deliberately displaces the feet from one track to two, three or four tracks – that is, the tracks made by the individual feet – at the same time asking for bend or flexion through the body, and sending the horse sideways. Lateral work requires that the shoulders or the hindquarters are moved from straight, into the positioning (bend and/or flexion) necessary for the particular lateral movement required – leg yield, shoulder-fore, shoulder-in, travers, renvers, half-pass.

Before such work is contemplated, it's a good idea to have basic rhythm and balance established in all paces, as well as half-halts and the associated obedience to the driving and restraining aids, all with willingness and without tension. Your horse should be able to keep to a metronomic rhythm throughout work in walk, trot and canter before you embark on lateral work, because the initial introduction of lateral work can cause loss of all the foregoing, which is often the case with any new work. Obviously this is somewhat counter-productive, as lateral work is used to improve the engagement and the quality of the paces by engaging the hindlegs and having control of the shoulders, so having the basics in place helps a lot.

Although it is a sound policy to start lateral work in walk so that the horse has time to assimilate the information and execute the exercise, this doesn't mean that he is ready or able to carry out lateral work successfully without the above being in place.

Lateral work both needs, and improves, collection. It also encourages lateral and longitudinal suppleness and, done correctly, means that the horse will place the inside hindleg more and more under the centre of gravity, thus taking more weight behind to improve the strength and carrying power of the quarters. The work should be carried out on both reins, as the idea is that everything can be done with equal suppleness in both directions.

It's as important to be able to stop any lateral movement as it is to start it, so that the horse doesn't take over the sideways movement; it is equally important to come out of the lateral work and straighten the horse – aligning the shoulders to the quarters and not the other way round – before each and every corner. There are exceptions to this when working on specific remedial exercises using the corner to emphasize a point to the horse.

As a general rule, lateral work should be ridden from one marker to another, so that you are disciplined in your approach right from the start. For example, if a trot or canter half-pass is required from K to G in the short arena, then you should leave the track at K and you shouldn't arrive at the centreline until just before G; if a half-pirouette in canter is asked for on the diagonal between M and X (as in PSG in the long arena), you come off at M, on the line to X, and return after the half-pirouette, still on the diagonal line, back towards M.

Preparing the horse on the short side of the arena with half-halts, and establishing and keeping the bend through the corner, or off a circle, makes the setting up (positioning) of lateral work much simpler for both horse and rider.

- The forwardness of the pace, its balance, rhythm and expression, are really important.

Once understood, it isn't the lateral exercise, of itself, which is important: it's how it is done that matters, as with most things in life.

In all work, but particularly in lateral work, it really matters that the rider remains in a central position in the saddle and considers carefully where his weight needs to be so that the horse is not hindered, or even prevented, from carrying out the movement. When a horse goes sideways, his outside leg has the furthest distance to travel, and any undue weight over that hindleg will cause a problem. The rider should therefore put slightly more weight on the inside seatbone, whilst remaining central, so that his inside leg can motivate the forward movement, and also so that the horse's inside hindleg doesn't take too big a sideways step, thus making it easier for his outside leg to come over.

This holds true for any work that requires the horse to step across with, or take weight on, the inside hindleg; if the rider keeps his own weight central but slightly over that inside hindleg, the load on the outside hindleg is lightened.

It's worth noting here that the main leg aid in lateral work is, in fact, the rider's *inside* leg, as that's the one that keeps the horse positioned correctly (together with the rein aids) and also keeps the impulsion and forwardness. The rider's outside leg initiates the sideways movement, and is there in case this needs to be reinforced from time to time; it shouldn't be necessary for this to be the dominant aid to push the horse sideways. However, this presupposes that the rider has both legs in contact with the horse so that both legs can give aids as necessary.

One often sees a rider sitting to the outside, away from the direction of travel, trying to shove the horse sideways with his outside leg – a nearly impossible task! In this instance, the rider is almost bound to have his inside leg away from the horse's side, because of his crooked position.

Trying to physically push the horse sideways with the leg quite simply doesn't work too well, wherever the rider sits – the aids need to be repeated rather than applied with a constant pressure, as this latter sort of aid doesn't work on two levels. First, the strength in the rider's leg muscles is likely to give out, and second, the horse will become completely dull to the leg aid.

The other thing that can happen is that the horse 'runs away' from the action of the rider's over-dominant outside leg; here the first thing to do is to reduce the influence of that outside leg, re-establish the forwardness with the inside leg and regain control of the sideways movement by going briefly into shoulder-in, and then ask again for the horse to go sideways.

A good thing to remember is that when you take your leg back actively behind the girth to give an aid, this 'talks' to the hindquarters and they will move away from that influence; the inside leg on the girth means go forwards and/or bend round it. The inside leg aid is really the key to successful lateral work as it gives the horse the impetus to keep forwards enough to perform the movement. Lateral work without sufficient forward tendency looks dreadful, and doesn't improve the quality of the pace, or the balance and the suppleness that lateral work is supposed to demonstrate.

The outside rein controls the speed and the degree of forwardness and bend; the inside rein controls the bend or flexion and the suppleness; both reins control the shoulders. Mirrors and a watchful trainer are more than useful when riding lateral work.

Turn on the Forehand

This basic exercise can be a good introduction to lateral work as it teaches the horse to move away from the influence of the rider's inside leg (displacing the quarters) without the added complication of keeping the trot or canter going forwards. It is done from walk.

Turn on the forehand is best done in an area where the wall can help to back the horse off and encourage him to turn.

How To Do It

Take an inside track (on the left rein) down the long side (leave enough room for the horse's head and neck to move round without hitting the wall, so about 1.5–2m in from the track). Establish halt at a marker; change your whip from the left hand into the right hand; position your horse to the right (this is now your inside rein); put your weight slightly on to your inside seatbone without compromising your central position or leaning forwards; then, with your right leg a bit behind the girth, push the quarters over until you've changed direction (180 degrees – roughly six steps); your left hand is half-halting to prevent the horse from moving forwards. Ride a step at a time so the horse doesn't whizz round, using your outside (left) leg to prevent this.

Ultimately, you want your horse to step round the forehand with the hindlegs. Ideally he shouldn't make any ground forwards, but should step up and down with the inside foreleg (right leg) while the outside foreleg moves round the inside leg, in the rhythm of the walk. If your horse resists the inside leg aid, a light tapping with the whip can be of considerable use.

It's a good idea to halt your horse on the straight for a couple of seconds after completing a turn on the forehand, so he learns not to dash off. If the turn has been done well, you should find that your horse halts well, too – a side benefit of turn on the forehand.

Turn on the Forehand into Rein-back

There is another aspect to this exercise. There's a point about half way through the turn when the horse will often offer a few steps backwards. Within the turn this is not at all what is wanted, *but* it's also a good way into the rein-back and is often used to teach this. If rein-back is on your agenda, allow a few steps back, using the word 'back' if you like, then go forwards again and complete the turn. Intersperse this work with turns on the forehand that have no element of rein-back, so that, as usual, your horse learns to wait to see what you want.

LATERAL WORK

Leg Yield

The first and most basic lateral movement is leg yield. It can be used to teach and/or refresh your horse's understanding of obedience to your leg aids to go sideways whilst keeping the forward tendency. It's a suppling exercise on four tracks, as opposed to a collecting exercise, and thus very useful in the warm-up. It is highly useful to teach the young horse acceptance of the forwards and sideways aids, and for the advanced horse as a loosening and suppling exercise.

In leg yield, the horse remains straight throughout the length of his body with a very slight, hardly discernible, *flexion* at the poll (not neck bend) away from the direction of travel, and the inner legs cross over and in front of the outer legs. It's important that the quarters do not lead in this movement, so if anything, the shoulders should be marginally in front but the horse should be as parallel to the track as is feasible.

Leg yield to the right away from the rider's left leg, with slight flexion left.

How To Do It

Leg yield can be ridden in walk, trot and canter, and is asked for in trot at Elementary level in the UK.

On the left rein, turn the horse on to the three-quarter line after A or C. Ride him straight for a couple of strides so that you're sure that the quarters are aligned behind the shoulders.

Then for leg yield to the right, use your left leg at the girth, with your right leg in a supporting role just behind the girth. Take up the left rein, just enough to get a slight flexion to the left by turning your wrist inwards; the right rein needs to allow this flexion without losing control of the horse's shoulders. Then ride the horse on as parallel a line as you can both manage towards the outside track. Reward any effort the horse makes to do this.

Don't overdo the sideways: take maybe half the length of the school to get to the track – choosing an arena marker towards which to ride is a good way to do this, otherwise you risk teaching the horse to fall through the right shoulder, and the benefit of leg yield is lost. If you find that your horse is going sideways too quickly, use both legs to ride him forwards out of it and then try leg yield again; don't just let him drift to the track as he chooses.

When the above exercise is working well, take the horse on the left rein down the centreline at A, keeping the left flexion you'll have from the turn; set him up with a half-halt; put a little more weight on your right seatbone, with your left leg a little behind the girth to drive in the rhythm of the pace, forwards and sideways (to the right); your right leg controls the sideways steps and also helps to keep the forward movement. Ride from D to M, which is quite steep enough initially. Using the markers helps

you to keep the emphasis on forwards first and sideways second.

You could also do as above, but change the flexion from left to right as you get on to the centreline and then leg yield away from your right leg.

● The difficult bit is that you need to do all the above more or less simultaneously, which tends to be true of everything you do on a horse.

Leg yield can be ridden from the inside track to the track; from the centreline to the track, or vice versa; with the horse's head to the wall, or the quarters to the wall – in each case the angle should be not more than 45 degrees. It can be ridden, shallowly or steeply, across the arena on a long or short diagonal, on a loop, or out of the corner; it can also be ridden on the circle line to good effect, spiralling in and out from a large to a smaller circle.

LEFT: *Leg-yield exercise on a 5m loop.*

BELOW: *Leg yield spiralling in on a circle.*

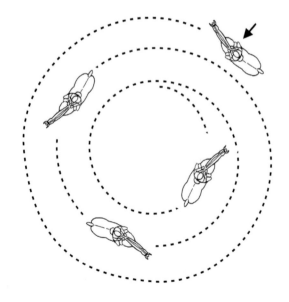

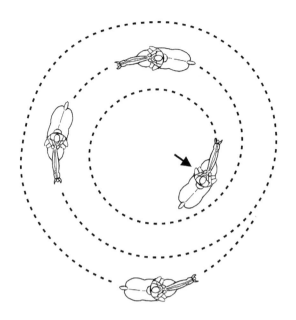

Leg yield spiralling out on a circle.

Leg yield: head to the wall on the left rein, away from rider's right leg.

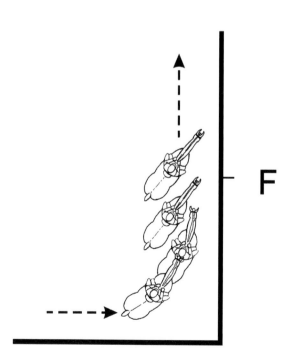

Leg yield: head to the wall on the left rein, away from rider's right leg.

In a zig-zag pattern, ride the horse on the left rein in leg yield from the centreline towards the half-marker; after 5m, straighten up by aligning the shoulders with the quarters, ride one straight stride, then re-position into leg yield back towards the centreline; on the centreline, one straight stride, and off you go the other way. To begin with, be satisfied with a zig, a zag and possibly another zig; eventually, challenge yourself by how many you can fit in (obviously this is easier in a long arena).

The following is another good, but quite difficult exercise: instead of riding a 'proper' corner on the left rein through the short side with the usual inside flexion, take the inside track (about 1.5–2m in from the long side), put your horse into outside flexion with the outside (right) rein (thus making your right leg the inside leg), put your left leg back a little from the girth into support position, right leg just behind the girth to push the quarters sideways, and send the horse sideways down the long side (not so close to the wall that he hits his nose on it and backs off – give him plenty of room), on not more than a 45-degree angle to the wall.

Take care to keep the flexion slight (not to have too much inside neck bend) as this will encourage your horse to fall out through the left shoulder and you won't achieve leg yield. In this leg yield, proceed down the long side, and at some point, execute a turn on the forehand – and thus a change of rein. The finished product should be that your horse is at a 45-degree angle with his head to the wall, ready to leg yield the other way.

Faults include falling out through the outside shoulder; losing the rhythm and forward

tendency of the pace; tension in the rider, resulting in tension through the horse; too much sideways and not enough forwards travel; and the rider sitting off to one side, usually away from the direction of travel.

Leg yield helps to promote suppleness and teaches the horse that leg aids can mean sideways as well as forwards – the beauty of leg yield is that it can be taught at an early stage to any horse and used throughout the training to the highest level in all three paces. Remember that leg yield requires a straight horse with slight flexion away from the direction of travel.

Shoulder-fore and Shoulder-in

These movements can be ridden in walk and trot on three tracks. Shoulder-fore normally comes before shoulder-in because it has a lesser angle and bend, and both can be ridden in canter as well (when they become straightening exercises). These exercises are easier for the rider to learn in walk, but usually easier for the horse to perform in trot. Both help to engage the inside hindleg, enabling the horse to step more under the centre of gravity, thus setting him on the path towards collection and self-carriage because of the increased lateral and longitudinal suppleness that develops as a result of a correctly ridden movement. However, the forwardness of the trot should *not* be compromised.

Shoulder-in left on three tracks; outside hind leg; inside hindleg and outside foreleg; inside foreleg.

The theory behind these exercises is that the hips are square to the track, and the shoulders are taken in off the track to create the desired three tracks (the outside hindleg on its own track, the inside hindleg and outside foreleg on the same track, and the inside foreleg on its own track); the horse is correspondingly bent to the inside and sent down the 'line' away from the direction of the bend. If the degree of angle is too deep, the horse tends to become unbalanced and wobbly, and his hips won't be square to the track, so the suppling and collecting elements of the movement are compromised. An important element of this is that the front legs should be crossing.

How To Do It

It is easier to start shoulder-fore or shoulder-in without any bend at all so that your horse has a straight neck and stays on the outside rein, before you attempt to put bend into the equation. So you ride what is almost leg yield (without any flexion) with the shoulders off the track so you get the feel of that first.

A good way of maintaining the idea of moving the shoulders is to go, on the left rein, on to a line off the outside track with your horse straight. Then move the shoulders slightly to the left, keeping the quarters on this line, and go down the line for several strides. Move the shoulders back into alignment with the quarters so that the horse is straight again, and repeat the exercise as often as you can, depending upon the length of the arena, and ride through the corner as usual. This exercise establishes that you know how to, and can, move the shoulders whilst keeping the quarters square to whatever line you are on.

Another more complex but useful exercise is to start on the outer track, moving only the shoulders, again with no neck bend, on to an inner track, and move along this track for a couple of strides keeping parallel to the outer track. Then, with your outside leg and inside rein, move the whole horse on to a new track, keeping the positioning of the shoulders, for a couple of strides. Move over again on to a third track, and so on, across the arena. So you are riding a series of stepped exercises, keeping the shoulders in advance.

When you can do this, put in the positioning – the bend round the rider's inside leg and flexion to the inside – which is the final piece of the shoulder-in jigsaw: at this point the effect of better engagement starts to come in.

LEFT: *Correct left shoulder-in.*

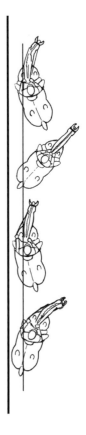

RIGHT: *From the top: travers right, too much neck bend for balance. Leg yield. Neither one thing nor the other! Shoulder-in, too much neck bend.*

This is all to prevent either excessive neck bend to the inside with the shoulders still firmly on the track, or 'bum out', where the quarters are allowed to escape to the outside. *Neither of these is shoulder-in.*

Set up the shoulder-in through a corner, or ride a small circle (8–10m), making sure that the horse accepts the inside flexion and moves round the rider's inside leg and is in the outside rein. If so, good; if not, ride the circle once more, and then again, until this is the case.

As you come on to, or back to, the track, half-halt with the outside rein, keep the shoulders on the circle line and the inside flexion from the corner or circle. Use your inside leg to maintain the bend and the forward movement, with your outside leg passively behind the girth to control

 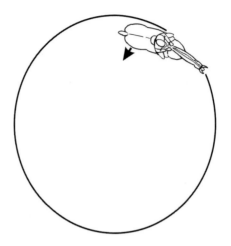

Work on the circle – shoulder-in and travers.

the quarters, and send the horse down the track, bent away from the direction of movement with the shoulders clearly off the track. You should be looking straight ahead down the line of travel. *This is shoulder-in.* Shoulder-in is the only lateral exercise where the horse is bent away from the direction of travel (leg yield doesn't count).

A visual image that can be useful is to imagine someone walking on the track by the horse's outside shoulder – shoulder-in would give that person room to do so without being flattened. (Thanks to Paul Fielder for this tip.)

Travers

Travers is, simply, 'quarters in' off the track, with slightly more bend than shoulder-in maintained to the inside; if you like, it is more or less the opposite to shoulder-fore and shoulder-in where the shoulders are brought in off the track: this time, the hindlegs cross and the horse is bent in the direction of travel. Travers can be ridden in all three paces.

With travers, the shoulders and front legs should stay straight on the track while the quarters are displaced inwards off the track to make a deeper angle of four tracks. However, if the angle is too deep, the horse can't keep the

shoulders square to the track, and the balance, regularity and fluency of the pace will be lost, as will the efficacy of the movement.

How To Do It

Travers requires the quarters to be displaced to the inside track, as we've said. It also requires positioning – flexion and bend. However, initially, trying to put all this in place in one go isn't likely to work, and both horse and rider will end up feeling stressed. So, as before, start with a shallow leg yield in walk on the left rein with the horse's head towards the wall, with barely any flexion, and the quarters slightly in off the track.

Another exercise to try in walk is to ride a few leg-yielding strides along the wall, then ask the horse to do a turn on the forehand to change the rein; do a few strides of leg yield, then another turn. This exercise helps the horse understand the influence of the rider's outside leg.

When the horse accepts the outside leg aid and yields to it easily, staying in with his quarters (ideally, you want four-track or 30 degrees of angle), change the flexion and turn the movement into travers. Before the horse comes up with any objections, revert to leg yield and repeat until this exercise flows easily –

which can take a while – but it will pay dividends when he accepts the change of flexion within a good forward working trot.

When this is going well, try this next exercise: on a 20m circle in trot to the left, set up the positioning that you've achieved in the earlier exercises – a slight flexion to the inside on the track of the circle (head, neck and shoulders stay on the circle line); then displace the quarters to the inside of the circle with your outside leg, but with care so the horse remains balanced. Don't over-position the horse to the inside with a strong inside rein: a slight flexion is all that is required, and you need to maintain a soft inside rein. Come into and out of the leg yield on the circle so your horse gets used to moving his shoulders and quarters on request. When your horse knows what's expected of him, make this exercise more taxing by using a 10m circle.

A really good suppling exercise, incorporating travers and shoulder-in, is to decrease the circle size with travers and increase it with shoulder-in. This is not the easiest, and needs care and precision.

So, to the finished movement: just as with shoulder-in, start out of a corner or from an 8–10m circle, with a half-halt to warn the horse that something is going to be happen; keep the horse's head, neck and shoulders on the track, ask for inside flexion with the rein in conjunction with the inside leg, use an active outside leg behind the girth to send the horse sideways from that leg with the quarters displaced to the inside – and you have travers.

To start with, the angle should not be more than the horse can maintain without tension or resistance, otherwise his balance will be compromised. Be satisfied with a few steps in a

LEFT: Left travers – four tracks.

RIGHT: Travers left down the long side, out of a 10m circle.

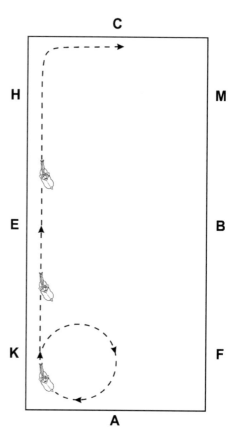

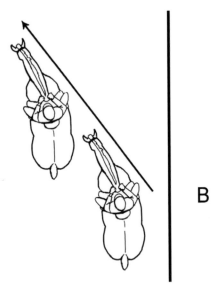

B

ABOVE: Travers left across the diagonal; preparation for half-pass; imagine the diagonal line moved to the left, and the movement would be renvers.

RIGHT: Renvers.

forward trot, and straighten him (shoulders to quarters, not the other way round) before he starts to struggle and slow down – send him forwards straight and praise him. Go back to the circle work to re-establish the bend, and try again on the track.

Travers is a great exercise down the long side after a well ridden corner to encourage your horse to maintain activity and energy, as the most common problems in lateral work are that the horse loses energy and slows down and stiffens against the aids. Horses generally find putting their quarters in much easier than taking their shoulders in, so travers can be most useful.

However, a cautionary note here. If your horse is already crooked to the extent that the quarters are always to the inside, then less travers and more shoulder-in would be indicated on that rein.

Travers on the diagonal is also an effective way to introduce the horse to half-pass; however, first the horse must learn to maintain energy by coming off the rider's inside leg whilst also obeying the rider's outside sideways pushing aid. Then if you ride a diagonal line, you need to imagine there's a wall on that line and align the horse accordingly, with the quarters displaced away from the imaginary wall. From there you need make only a slight adjustment to the parallel positioning, and you're in half-pass!

Renvers

Although this is not a movement asked for in tests, renvers is another most valuable suppling and collecting exercise. Here the hindlegs remain on the track and the forehand is displaced to the inside, but the horse moves into the direction of the bend (unlike shoulder-in).

If you change from travers to renvers on the same rein, because of the opposite bend the inside hindleg becomes the opposite one to that in travers. Thus the rider can work the hindlegs without changing the rein.

Travers and renvers are virtually the same movement, with the wall – either real or imagined – changed, as illustrated in the diagram of travers, and the photograph. The difference is more technical than actual, depending on the positioning of the horse in the arena. In travers the forelegs move along the track; in renvers the hindlegs move along the track. In simple terms, renvers is 'bum out' and travers is 'bum in'.

How To Do It

For renvers on the left rein, ride through the corner of the school as usual, with inside (left) flexion and bend. Ride the horse straight for a stride or two, then half-halt and take his shoulders on to the inner track, and bend and flex him to the outside (to the right), leaving the quarters on the track. You need to ride slightly off the track to accommodate this and to give the horse room to keep his quarters on the track.

Renvers can be especially useful if your horse has a tendency to fall out through the outside shoulder. By putting the horse into renvers you control the shoulders, and then by changing the flexion and bend to the inside, you can get an improved shoulder-in.

Ride shoulder-in, change the bend into renvers, change the bend again and move the quarters into travers, straighten and finish with shoulder-in. In this way, you can work the shoulders and the quarters, and in so doing, considerably improve the overall straightness of your horse (because you have control of, and can manoeuvre, both ends – using bend to straighten).

The following exercise (courtesy of Kyra Kyrklund) incorporates several of the lateral movements, and definitely tests the combination's ability and flexibility; it makes the rider concentrate on where exactly the horse's hindlegs are, and makes both horse and rider extremely agile mentally and physically. Further, it helps to improve the rider's ability to put the horse equally into both reins.

On the centreline, on the left rein, displace the right hindleg to the right, then put your horse on to that line in leg yield so that, effectively, you're riding a leg yield along the centreline with the hindlegs on one side of the line and the forelegs on the other side. After several leg-yielding strides, change the bend and flexion to the right so that the horse's head and neck are now positioned on the centreline with the ears parallel, into travers right. After several strides of that, change the bend and flexion to the left, and ride left shoulder-in; then straighten your horse and halt at G. You could, of course, go from travers, to renvers, to shoulder-in if you like a challenge!

When you've mastered this in walk, try it in trot, but you will need either a mirror or a trainer to help with this.

Half-pass

Whereas travers is normally asked for along the track, half-pass, as its name implies, is asked for across the arena. The steeper the half-pass across the diagonal, the more bend and engagement is required, so when it appears for the first time in a test at Medium level, it is usually done at a shallow angle with minimal bend and positioning. As the tests go up the scale, the angle required becomes more acute, until at Grand Prix it is at its most acute.

Like travers, half-pass can be ridden in all three paces, but in tests it is only asked for in trot and canter.

In trot half-pass, the horse needs to reach forwards with each stride, crossing his legs, outer in front of inner, at each stride. In canter this can't be done as the horse would fall over; here, the stride is opened and closed in a

*ABOVE: **Canter half-pass right.***

*LEFT: **Trot half-pass left.***

sideways action of the fore and hind limbs with each stride.

Half-pass is more or less travers across the diagonal but with the horse remaining more parallel to the track; if there has to be a compromise, then the shoulders may be very slightly in advance. It is never correct for the quarters to lead in half-pass.

How To Do It

For less experienced combinations embarking on half-pass, first make sure that both you and your horse are established in leg yield, shoulder-in and travers, on both reins. On a 20m circle in trot, make sure that you can change the flexion at the poll from left to right, regardless of the rein you are on. Do this slowly and deliberately so that you keep control of the shoulders and the hindlegs on the curve of the circle. Also check that you can do this on a straight line.

The following exercise can be useful: on the right rein, come through the corner on the short side on to the diagonal line, then change into left flexion and leg yield left towards the centre line; after several strides of leg yield, change the direction back to the long side but keep the left flexion and go in travers back to the track. This should be quite easy to do, because from the leg yield the horse is already encouraged to give in the ribcage to the rider's right leg, he is on the rider's left rein, and with the pull of the track, he should be willing to produce a first shallow half-pass/travers without tension or anxiety.

If any tension or resistance does creep in when riding half-pass, change immediately into leg yield, or put the horse on to a fairly small circle, re-establish balance and rhythm, and then try again.

Once this is successful, try the following: on the left rein, come off at the quarter marker in leg yield towards the centreline, then into shoulder-in left, then into left half-pass to the track; at the track change the bend and go immediately into right shoulder-in.

Another exercise is to ride a 10m circle, say on the left rein at H, in the long arena; at H,

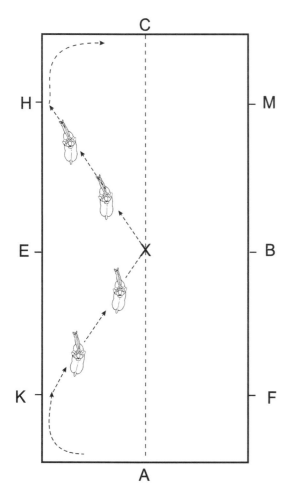

ABOVE: **Leg yield into travers.**

TOP RIGHT: **Half-pass left in trot, with good crossing and energy; it could have clearer positioning.**

BOTTOM RIGHT: **Half-pass left in trot, rear view, with clear positioning.**

after the circle, position the horse on the diagonal HXF with both his ears towards where he's going to go, and half-pass a few strides towards X; ride another 10m circle, set your horse up in travers and continue along the diagonal line towards F; if you can, move the shoulders over to the left in front of the quarters so that your horse is more parallel.

If this goes wrong, put him on to another 10m circle wherever you are on that diagonal, and try travers again; you can do this several times. This works well with horses that trail their quarters.

A variation of the above is useful for a horse that either lacks, or doesn't maintain, the correct bend in half-pass. From a 10m circle in trot, at H, take the horse in shoulder-in on to the diagonal line; ride a few strides in half-pass, then go further across the diagonal in shoulder-in; then half-pass, shoulder-in, and repeat until you reach the end of the diagonal line. If this isn't enough to sort out the correct bend, ride a 10m circle before each shoulder-in, making sure that you keep making progress across the diagonal line – this should remain your focus. This is because all half-passes are done on a diagonal line, and only the steepness of that line varies.

An exercise that leads well into the counter change of hand (*see* below) is to ride a half-pass left towards X; at X ride a 10m circle right; then go in half-pass right back to the track.

For better marks in the half-pass you need to put in more power for added lift and expression, so riding the half-pass in medium trot, and then back into more collection, gives you the flexibility to ask for more energy whenever you need it. Starting and finishing this exercise with a circle rebalances the horse, and in fact whenever his balance and engagement are compromised, ride a circle. However, in a test, make sure you keep the half-pass all the way to the track before straightening and re-bending to the new direction.

The Counter Change of Hand (Zig-Zag)

This is performed in half-pass at trot and canter, and is simply half-pass one way with an immediate change into half-pass the other way. In trot it is acceptable to show a couple (but no more!) of straight strides between each change

---

IMPORTANT POINTS TO REMEMBER

- Whatever the lateral work, it's very important to keep firmly in mind that it should be, first and foremost, forwards and then sideways, and not the other way round!
- Interspersing lateral work with some extensions and giving plenty of rest breaks to allow muscles and brains to relax are essential to any training session.

---

of direction – however, simple is actually the one thing this movement is not, as it requires a good degree of suppleness, flexion and bend, together with total control of the shoulders and quarters, which takes much time and patience to produce. In addition, canter zig-zag of course requires a flying change upon each change of direction!

A good visual image for this movement comes from Swedish trainer Major Wikne, via Inger Bryant. From half-pass left, as you start to change the bend for right half-pass, think about there being a tree round which you have to go without letting the quarters hit the tree (if you have more than one zig-zag, you'll need to visualize more than one tree).

PIROUETTES

Pirouettes are included in this chapter because there is a considerable element of lateral work in setting up these movements.

A full pirouette is only ridden in canter, from Intermédiare I to Grand Prix. Neither full nor half pirouettes are performed in trot (although there is always an exception, which in this case is in the Freestyle to Music at Intermédiare II and Grand Prix where pirouettes can be ridden in piaffe). Demi (half)-pirouettes are asked for in walk; they start at novice and the degree of difficulty increases through the levels to advanced in terms of the size required in the turn. At Prix St Georges there is a requirement for a demi-pirouette at canter.

Walk pirouette work can begin with a young horse as long as the understanding of basic training is established. However, work towards canter pirouettes is much more strenuous, mentally and physically, and would normally only commence when the horse is sufficiently balanced and strong from all the work that has gone before. A full canter pirouette is a very small circle on two tracks, with the forehand turning around the hindquarters through 360 degrees and taking between six and eight steps to complete.

The activity and rhythm of the canter – the regular three-beat rhythm – into and out of the pirouette should not be compromised; however, it has now been firmly established (scientifically, with the aid of gait analysis and modern frame-by-frame cameras) that the canter goes to four-time within the pirouette turn itself – if it didn't, the horse would, quite simply, fall over. (Grand Prix riders and trainers have known this for a long time, by the simple expedient of common sense!)

In canter pirouette the hindlegs shouldn't move either sideways or backwards. The inside hindleg forms the centre of the pirouette and shouldn't deviate from its position: it should mark time, up and down, in the rhythm of the canter each time it leaves the ground, with the size of the pirouette as small as the horse's balance will allow (though better a slightly larger correct pirouette than a smaller, incorrect one).

It follows that a half-pirouette has similar requirements, but the turn is made through 180 degrees and is, in effect, a change of rein within three to four steps. Any lateral, sideways, steps into or out of the pirouette would be considered incorrect.

The FEI and BD definitions are exactly the same: 'The pirouette is a circle executed on two tracks, with the radius equal to the length of the horse, the forehand round the haunches.'

General Principles of Pirouettes

The horse is bent and positioned in the direction of movement, with flexion to the inside, bringing the shoulders into the turn. The rider sits centrally but with more weight on the inside seatbone; the inside leg acts at the girth using light driving aids to keep the horse forwards; the outside leg is positioned slightly behind the girth, initially in a supporting role to keep the horse's outside leg stepping round the inside hindleg for the first step, then taking up a more dominant role so that the horse completes the movement. Both the rider's hands should move towards the inside, without pulling backwards on the reins, to facilitate the turning of the horse's shoulders. The steps should be deliberate, and the horse shouldn't swivel or pivot, or rush round.

Sitting 'away' from the movement, with your outside shoulder back – advocated by some trainers – works against the principle that your shoulders and hips should be aligned with the horse's shoulders and hips. You run the risk of being behind the movement, and more or less forcing the horse to step out to counter your shift in balance. You can, however, also turn your body too much to the inside, thus sending your weight to the outside, which will have a similar effect of unbalancing your horse. It is therefore always best to aim for a central position – and do look where you are going, so you keep on the line from whence you came.

Walk Pirouettes

The fluency of the walk, and the four-beat rhythm, should be maintained throughout the turn, with just enough forward movement so that the shoulders can turn round the quarters;

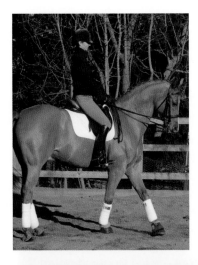

*Demi-pirouette
right in walk.*

too much tightness in the rein can result in a turn about the centre, as the forwardness of the walk has been stifled.

To begin with, walk pirouettes are performed on the track; as the work progresses through the levels, they are asked for off the track across the arena. In these early stages, 'large' half-pirouettes should be the norm to keep the all-important forward tendency at the forefront of both the rider's and the horse's mind. In a test, however, a 'large' half-pirouette should have a radius of not more than 1m of forward progress.

How To Do It

At the start of pirouette work, an easy way into what can potentially be a difficult movement is to ride quarter-pirouettes, either individually or as part of a sequence within a square. Practise shortening and lengthening the walk steps, using half-halts, before you attempt the quarter-pirouettes.

Set up a square in the arena, using poles or cones, so that you have a square of 15m or 20m, reducing to 12m, and then 10m as you progress. Walk across the square, and just before the track, half-halt on the outside rein to indicate that something is going to happen and to adjust (shorten) the step length. Think of taking the shoulders round the turn, bending the horse round your inside leg, supporting with the outside leg so that the quarters don't swing out, guiding him with your inside rein, with the outside rein limiting the amount of neck bend but 'giving' enough to allow the turn, so that you describe a quarter of a small circle. Remember that the outside shoulder has further to go than the inside one, so the horse needs enough room to do this without resistance. It can be most helpful to use a bit of pressure with your outside knee to help the horse understand that he should bring his shoulders through – and remember to keep your body turning in line with his.

Then ride straight again across your square and repeat the aids at each turn. The smaller the square, the tighter the turns will have to be.

Eventually you should be able to execute a quarter turn (pirouette) anywhere you like.

When this is established, you can try a half turn – through 180 degrees – to change the rein, but you need to feel that the shoulders turn round the quarters without the quarters being pushed away or stepping out, and without the walk sequence and quality being lost. Your horse should not stop walking at any point.

It can be useful to think (only think, don't do!) about the first step of the half-pirouette as shoulder-in, half-pass for the second and third steps, and then straightening into the final step so that the horse doesn't go laterally back to the track. Too much outside leg, too soon, just makes the horse step sideways and cross behind, a serious mistake, and this can lead to the horse sticking and pivoting round his inside hindleg, so that the walk sequence is lost – *the most serious mistake.* Here, someone watching from the ground is really valuable.

Another way into pirouette work is to develop it from shoulder-fore. On a 10m circle,

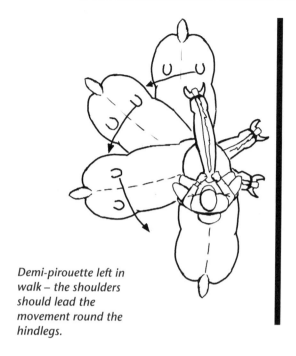

Demi-pirouette left in walk – the shoulders should lead the movement round the hindlegs.

take up a shoulder-fore position, then reduce the size of that circle keeping the shoulders in advance, until the horse is describing a really rather small circle. Do this gradually, and use some forward riding out of it to refresh the energy, before trying again. (This works well in walk and in canter.)

If the walk steps before the half-pirouette are too long, it will be difficult to keep the regularity of the pace within the confines of the pirouette, as the steps do need to shorten within the movement – and the walk before and after the half-pirouette is as important as the movement. This is not to suggest that the horse should be slowed down to a crawl, but rather that he learns to adjust the length of the walk step as part of the training in the walk.

It is important to finish off the pirouette on the same line as you went into it, whether that's carrying on across the arena with a turn on to the long side, or making sure there are no lateral steps back to the track if doing the demi-pirouette on the track. This latter problem will be exaggerated if you've made the movement so big that you are nowhere near the track! It is not a lateral movement, and so the rules of keeping the horse tracking straight apply.

The most common faults are a reluctance to turn at all; losing the bend; sideways or backward steps behind; losing the forwardness; the inside hindleg sticking or pivoting; losing the walk sequence; stopping completely; coming against the hand; and general tension and resistance.

At the higher levels, collected walk is required sometimes before, and always between, two half-pirouettes – hence the necessity to be able to shorten the walk steps.

Developing Canter Pirouettes

The German Grand Prix rider/trainer, Hubertus Schmidt, is *the* acknowledged expert in training and riding exemplary pirouettes. He has trained many horses to Grand Prix, and the canter pirouettes are the highlight of his tests.

This stems from his gradual and progressive build-up towards what is extremely demanding work for the horse, both mentally and physically, requiring the highest degree of collection since in its finished form it is executed as nearly as possible on the spot.

We therefore present the techniques he teaches, from various articles, from his presentation at the Global Dressage Forum in Holland, the British Dressage National Convention, and his seminars elsewhere in the world, on just this subject.

Hubertus concentrates on the quality of the canter, its consistent rhythm and 'throughness' on both reins, together with correct flexion and

LEFT: *Correct bend into a right canter pirouette.*

BELOW: *The beginning of a left canter pirouette showing clear positioning.*

bending, and the ease of transitions to and from walk. He then adds half-pass on both reins, riding in a shortened canter and then increasing the length of the stride within the half-pass, with the horse remaining relaxed and supple to both reins. This teaches the horse to maintain the bend and to move sideways in the direction of the bend, both essential for pirouette work.

He works on a 20m circle, shortening and lengthening the canter strides, ensuring that there is no loss of rhythm or impulsion. If the horse becomes too high in the neck, or stiffens against the shortening, Hubertus takes him into a lower outline to counteract this tendency. The horse must stay straight on this bent line, with quarters neither in nor out, and make the shorter strides within this straightness. As this work progresses, it can be that the horse loses some of the 'jump' in the canter and goes rather flat; this is a compromise that Hubertus feels is acceptable until the horse can easily shorten, carry weight behind, with good activity, and then regain the jump, so that he can collect as much as will be required in the pirouettes. This is a crucial step, because if this is not truly established, the pirouettes will not come good; therefore it should be revisited as often as necessary.

The above can take quite a long time, but Hubertus doesn't move on until it is firmly established. Equally, he doesn't attempt any work towards the working pirouette if the horse is too strong in the hand, or isn't consistent to the flexion and bend, or isn't 'sitting' enough. *He goes back to a point where the work is correct, and then moves forwards again.*

The circle is decreased to 12m, and then to a 10m volte, with his horse completely straight and aligned, in shoulder-fore, on the circle line. This increases the degree of weight to be taken by the inside hindleg. The horse must be upright to the outside rein so that the rider can collect him on this rein for the shortened strides; the horse should be light on the inside rein as this works with the inside leg on the same side, and if the contact on the inside rein is too strong, the inside hind steps short and thus will not 'jump' forwards sufficiently to carry weight.

From there, he starts to turn the horse's shoulders round the hindlegs into a large working pirouette. The rider's inside leg keeps the horse jumping forwards and prevents the radius of the circle from becoming too small, as the horse will often try to do this to avoid carrying weight. To clarify this point, the steps should be kept small but the working pirouette should remain large.

Eventually this work can be done on a 5–6m volte, at which point, if the horse remains in balance, Hubertus tries a half-pirouette or even a whole one. This can only work if the horse remains good in the hand and keeps the quality of the canter; if either of these elements is lost, then the rider should go back to the level the horse can cope with. This is especially important if the horse has a tendency to want to swivel round – to plant his inside hindleg and do a series of jumps around it, without this leg maintaining its step of the canter sequences.

Hubertus doesn't follow the general trend of using travers to teach pirouettes: he prefers to use shoulder-fore or shoulder-in. He feels that encouraging the horse to step to the inside with the hindlegs, as in travers, leads to the likelihood that the horse will step too much to the side and can thus avoid taking weight on the inside hindleg. Equally, the horse can easily become crooked and jump round, rather than keeping the canter sequence.

Until he can control all eight strides within the working pirouette, Hubertus doesn't take the pirouette any tighter, and if at any time the horse loses impulsion, he takes the working pirouette bigger again to remedy this.

As mentioned before, this work can take quite a few weeks, and it is also good to remember that this work is very strenuous for the horse and, come to that, for the rider. Plenty of rest breaks will ease the severity of the work.

Half-pirouette left in canter.

Working Half-pirouette on the Diagonal

A half-pirouette in canter on both reins is required at Prix St Georges. As before, the quality of the canter and the suppleness of the bend are paramount; the positioning through the corner should mean that the bend is already set up and the inside hindleg should be well under the centre of gravity. If all is in place, bringing the shoulders round 180 degrees, with the canter forward enough for the horse's balance, should be relatively straightforward.

Most riders tend to make the mistake of doing the first half of a half-pirouette too big and the second half too small; this is the usual cause of the horse losing balance. Doing it the other way round, with the first half smaller than the second half, works much better; four strides of canter should be enough to return you to the line from which you came. It works quite well to pin your eyes on the marker you came from as you're riding the half-pirouette, as that should help you to ride directly back to it; this also tends to make the size of the pirouette tighter, because you go where you look.

- An aside here about this movement: quite often people take too long to collect and position their horses for the half-pirouette, and in the process, do it way past X; this isn't correct, and you will lose marks.

Full Pirouettes

Although we said we wouldn't get into Grand Prix training, with pirouettes it is hard not to go just a few more steps!

When everything is consistently in place, full pirouettes can be ridden on the diagonal and on the centreline. An eight-stride pirouette has the advantage of giving both horse and rider the time and balance to produce a good movement. Although six strides are allowed, this often leads to making the final steps too quick, with the radius too small, as the horse

Lateral Work and Pirouettes • 123

loses his balance and the jump quality of the canter suffers. The rider needs to retain the ability to increase the radius of the circle at will in order to keep the quality of the pace, and this depends, crucially, on control of the shoulders.

If a patient, logical progression of training is followed, and the horse is confident and understanding of the aids, pirouettes can be most useful in teaching increased engagement or weight carrying of the hindlegs, together with a general improvement in suppleness.

Half and full pirouettes are all about moving the horse's shoulders around the hindlegs within the rhythm and sequence of the canter. Further, the development of the lowering of the hindquarters is what is required, together with the mobility of the shoulders.

● The canter before, during and after the pirouette should keep the same high quality.

If the collection is correct, then thinking more about the pace than the movement, and allowing the horse to do what you have asked, is better than trying to over-dominate everything he does. Sometimes there can be too much support: the horse does need to do it himself! Then the half and full pirouettes look effortless, despite the amount of technique, muscle power and strength needed.

Full pirouette left in canter – please imagine the last three strides! Judy Harvey (GB) and Fitzcerraldo.

13 'Give and Retake' and Rein-Back

No philosophers so thoroughly comprehend us as dogs and horses.

Herman Melville

'Give and retake' and rein-back are subject to a great deal of misinterpretation, so we hope we can make both terms clearer and more easily understood.

'GIVE AND RETAKE' (*ÜBERSTREICHEN*)

The FEI *Dressage Handbook* gives the following definition:

> The brief release of the contact, wherein the rider in one clear motion extends the hand/s forward along the crest of the horse's neck and then rides for several strides without contact. Its purpose is to demonstrate that, even with loose reins, the horse maintains its carriage, balance, pace and tempo.

The British Dressage rule book states:

> The rider pushes forwards one or both hands as stated on the test sheet to clearly release the contact and then retake it. The movement of the hand/s should be continuous and achieved over two or three strides. As this is a test of self-carriage the horse should stay in balance, keeping the same rhythm, level of engagement, suppleness of the back and accept the restoration of contact without any loss of submission.

Usually the requirement is for both hands to release the contact. Give and retake can be requested on a circle, over the centreline, or on a diagonal. On occasion there is a requirement for only one hand to go forwards, and that is always the inside hand; this is usually on a circle so the rider can show that the horse is securely in the outside rein and upright to it.

To be totally clear, it's not enough to push both hands up the neck without relinquishing the contact – the contact must be released completely so that both the reins are clearly looped.

It is unnecessary and undesirable to lean forwards while this is happening, as this will totally unbalance the horse just at the moment when you are trying to demonstrate how well balanced he is, and that he doesn't need the reins to maintain that balance! It's not the best idea to open your fingers and let the reins slip through – if your horse decides to make a bid for freedom, you might be out of the arena by the time you've regained control!

The only thing that should marginally change is that your horse pushes his nose slightly forward of the vertical. He should look as though the contact is still there – so if he falls in a heap on his forehand, loses his balance, hollows, sticks his head in the air, hurries or loses his rhythm, there is still work to be done.

Give and re-take in canter left: (a) The reins are taken up the neck but the contact is not relinquished; (b) the reins are clearly in loops, so contact is relinquished. (The rider's arm position is exaggerated to make the loops clearly visible.)

Fundamentally, the give and retake is a test of the correct way of going.

REIN-BACK

The FEI defines rein-back as follows:

> The rein-back is a rearward diagonal movement with a two-beat rhythm but without a moment of suspension. Each diagonal pair of legs is raised and returned to the ground alternately, with the forelegs aligned on the same track as the hindlegs.
>
> During the entire exercise, the horse should remain 'on the bit', maintaining its desire to move forwards.

The British Dressage rule book describes rein-back thus:

> The rein-back is an equi-lateral retrograde movement in which the feet are raised and set down by diagonal pairs. The feet should be well raised and the hind feet remain well in line.
>
> At the preceding halt, as well as during the rein-back, the horse, although standing motionless and moving backwards respectively, should remain on the bit, maintaining his desire to move forwards.

● Since rein-back is not a movement natural to the horse, and many horses exhibit great anxiety when asked to go backwards, it is very important not to pull back via the reins, or to force the horse back in an insensitive way.

Unlike the walk, which is a four-beat pace, the rein-back is two-beat with the legs in diagonal pairs, like the trot but without the moment of suspension – but it certainly looks like walk! It demonstrates obedience and suppleness, and when correctly done promotes and demonstrates the 'throughness' of the horse. As the joints of the hindlegs are encouraged to bend more, this helps with collection by putting the horse more on the hindleg – that is, taking more weight behind. Conversely, without the ability to 'sit' and take some weight behind, a correct rein-back is very difficult to achieve.

The more against the hand, or behind the bit, the horse becomes, the less able he will be to execute a correct rein-back. In order for the rein-back to be successfully executed the horse needs to stand with equal weight over all four legs, in a square halt, and remain on the aids, with a rounded, relaxed back. The rider gives a small aid to move forwards with seat and leg, but at the same time, half-halts and takes the rein to prevent the forward movement. If the horse understands these conflicting aids, he will offer to step back.

Be very happy with one or two offered steps, and praise him effusively. This is not the moment to worry about the horse going crooked in the rein-back; that can be sorted out when he understands the exercise and carries it out willingly.

Initially it can be helpful to have a person on the ground who places a hand on the horse's chest, or taps very lightly on the chest or the legs with a whip, to indicate that he should step backwards. If you've taught your horse to go backwards away from you in the stable with your voice, or when leading him, this can come into play with great effect. Praise and reward are good in this context.

Rein-back can also be taught from a turn on the forehand, where the horse is asked to go back for a couple of steps just on the point of turning. You can ride this from leg yield along the wall, as described in Chapter 12, or simply ride down the long side. Go on to the inner track, and make a turn back on yourself into the wall, using turn on the forehand. At the half-way stage, just as the horse is beginning to cross his legs behind to start the turn on the forehand, ask for a couple of steps backwards. Be content with even a half step back to begin with, until your horse understands what is required, but intersperse this with a complete turn on the forehand sometimes so that he keeps listening to what you want and doesn't take over the movement.

It can be useful to slightly lighten the seat (but not by leaning forwards) to free up the horse's back. Some riders put both their legs slightly further back behind the girth when giving the aid, to make it as clear as possible to the horse that something different is being requested. There should be a light asking with the reins, and when the rein-back is offered, the hands should stay quiet. Ideally, when the rein-back is happening, the rider should be able to sit quiet, doing nothing other than asking for, and counting, the necessary number of steps back.

The aids need to be changed on the last but one rein-back step wanted, so that the horse understands to go immediately, but not hurriedly, forwards. There should be no hesitation or halt between rein-back and the forward transition – so if you want five steps back, the aid to go forwards would be applied on the fourth backward step.

When (note 'when' and not 'if'!) the horse goes crooked, it can help to bring the forehand back into line by taking both reins to the side on which he has gone crooked, and moving the shoulders over the same way; in other words, if the quarters swing to the right, take the forehand the same way and in so doing, realign your horse.

A good rein-back has the following qualities:

● The horse is 'on the aids', and 'through' from behind to the bit
● The steps back are clearly defined in a diagonal two-beat rhythm
● The diagonal legs are clearly lifted and put down
● The horse is quiet in the contact, with the mouth closed
● He is supple, obedient, relaxed…
● …straight, calm and steady…

● ...and ready to go forwards immediately into whatever pace is required

Using your voice can be very helpful in training, but muttering the word 'back' during a rein-back at C will earn you a reprimand (and a loss of marks) from the judge, should you be heard.

When things go wrong, the horse makes his unwillingness quite clear to anyone watching by a variety of the following resistances: he becomes crooked, hollow, resistant, reluctant, hesitant, drags his feet, breaks the diagonal, or is wide behind. He comes behind the aids, behind the vertical and opens his mouth; in the extreme he will refuse to move or will rear, and will generally indicate his total lack of submission (and perhaps understanding).

Horses sometimes use rein-back (or just going backwards, actually) to get away from the rein contact – this can vary from a couple of steps to rushing backwards across the arena! Hold your nerve and keep the rein contact (don't pull), and either let him work out for himself that the contact is still there, which usually results in him going forwards again, or, when he does stop, ask for even more rein-back, and then ask him to go forwards.

In our experience, rein-back does nothing to put a horse 'on the bit': rather, the horse already needs to be 'on the bit' before a correct rein-back can be achieved. However, as above, it can be useful to use on occasion to reinforce obedience when the horse tries to take over control.

If he hollows, pulling back more strongly on the reins will just make things worse. It's a good idea to bear in mind that when a horse puts his head up and hollows his back, the withers drop, the back becomes concave and the hindlegs move out behind. From this position, a horse really can't do what you want, however much you haul, and all you succeed in doing is making his back and mouth thoroughly uncomfortable. He won't be able to bend and lift his hindlegs, so the more you pull, the more resistance you will encounter, and the best you can hope for is that he goes backwards with his hindlegs splayed, and his feet dragging and out of sequence. You certainly won't get good marks, and you'll have 'taught' your horse that rein-back is unpleasant and painful.

In this instance, the best way to proceed is to go back to the beginning and ensure that the horse understands what is required via work on the ground or with an assistant; if his inclination is to hollow, a longer, deeper outline will go some way to counteract this while he is relearning how to go backwards.

The remedy to the above problems is, of course, to ensure that your horse is 'on the bit', with all that entails, and that he understands the movement so that he can react calmly and obediently to your aids.

Rein-back is a really useful gymnastic and balancing exercise, and it can also be used, as already mentioned, as an aid to obedience – but it still needs to be ridden correctly, whatever the provocation.

14 Changes

A canter is a cure for every evil.

(Benjamin Disraeli)

COUNTER CANTER

Counter canter is simply cantering along in one direction with the opposite, or 'wrong', canter lead, i.e. cantering with the right lead on the left rein. Given that a long time might have been spent establishing the canter with the 'correct' lead, horses may be forgiven if they

Right counter canter on the left rein; the rider is clearly using right canter aids with the horse flexed right over the leading leg. Pippa Fisher and Nadonna.

find this confusing. However, with the inherent crookedness of the horse and the tendency for canter often to show with the quarters to the inside – in other words, crooked – there's a compelling argument that counter canter can go a long way to straightening a horse.

Counter canter works towards keeping the horse more upright into the outside rein – as long as the bend over the leading leg is not so overdone that the quality of the canter is lost and the quarters have to move out to compensate for the overbending – and thus it is easier to keep the horse straight. The forehand and the quarters should stay on the same track, and the horse must be bent round the rider's inside leg in the direction of travel, so right bend in right canter, left bend in left canter, and bend over the leading leg in counter canter. It's quite interesting that riders often wildly overbend their horses in counter canter in an effort to keep in balance, when it would never occur to them to do so in 'normal' canter!

In the early stages of teaching counter canter, several things can be done to make the lesson easier for the horse to understand. These exercises are also good for teaching flying changes. Before asking the horse to go into counter canter, both horse and rider should be completely at ease with canter strike-offs on either rein. Changing the canter lead – left and right through trot, and then directly to and from walk (simple changes) – makes sure that the horse is on the aids, understands the aids for canter left and canter right, and is obedient to half-halts and transitions. These transitions can gradually come more quickly with fewer steps of trot or walk in between, as the horse's balance improves along with his understanding, and as the rider's ability improves.

Eventually the rider should be able to decide upon, and carry out, a specific number of strides between each change. For example, four canter strides then four walk then four canter, and so on, is challenging and very useful. However, it's amazing how quickly horses can start to anticipate, so be careful to mix this work, and the number of in-between strides you ask for, with other exercises.

Another dual-purpose exercise is to flex the horse right and left on a fairly large canter circle, without changing legs or doing any transitions, until he is quite comfortable and

WHAT IS DISUNITED?

Being disunited is when the horse changes legs in front or behind because he stiffens and loses his balance, without following through with the other legs; so for instance, he ends up with the right leg leading, but with the other three legs still in left canter. It looks uncomfortable, and it is, for both horse and rider. If this happens, just bring your horse back into trot, re-bend him and strike off again. Pulling him about will simply make him anxious and does nothing to help.

There's a school of thought that says push the horse on faster in the disunited canter and he'll change eventually; well, some do and some don't, but you might also either confuse him or turn him into a very hot – in both senses of the word – horse in the process! Quite often, keeping your horse in a slight shoulder-fore position means the problem doesn't come up. This also has the side-benefit of ensuring that the horse remains straight.

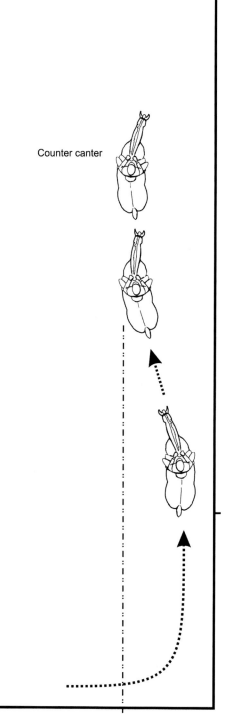

Counter canter

Shallow 5m loop as an introduction to counter canter right on the left rein.

balanced, whatever the leading leg and whatever the flexion. So to be clear, on a left circle change the flexion to the right (counter flexion) and back again, several times; this is necessarily done carefully and tactfully with the hands, as any change in the 'canter position' of the rider's seat and legs will at best have the horse doing a flying change to keep upright, or at worst he'll become disunited.

Working in a big space – a field or large arena – gives both horse and rider time to start counter-canter exercises, as above and as follows: ride through the short side of the arena in trot on the left rein, ride the corner as normal; take the horse into a 5m loop from the quarter marker, still in trot. Prepare the horse for right canter by half-halting and flexing to the right and ask for right canter; continue on the loop in counter canter and, a horse's length before the quarter marker, make a transition into trot so that you ride the corner in trot. Do the same again in the next corner so that the shape you ride is much like a bone.

This is a gentle introduction into counter canter which keeps the horse in balance and free from tension or anxiety. You can make the loop deeper, which increases the difficulty; you can also flatten out the loop, and in this process, aim for a more direct depart into counter canter.

When this is going well, you can abandon the loop and simply go for left canter, right canter, and so on around the arena, using transitions to and from trot, and then directly from walk, into canter, then walk (simple changes, *see* opposite).

The next stage is to make a large (say, 15m) half-circle towards the end of the arena with a very shallow angle back to the track, thus changing the rein, with a few strides of counter canter on the track before a transition to trot or walk before the corner. The half-circle can be gradually reduced in size, and the angle back to the track made steeper as the work progresses.

Right counter canter on the left rein through the corner.

(*See* the diagram 'diagonals and changes of rein', page 145.)

It is really important that the canter back towards the track stays in rhythm; the rider should think about shortening the strides slightly so that the horse stays in balance and off the forehand so that counter canter is possible, not forgetting the transition before the corner. What often happens instead is an increase in speed and in the length of the steps, so the counter canter is already in trouble and unbalanced, and the transition, usually to trot, is totally on the forehand.

When the horse is familiar with these exercises and can deal with them without tension, and without becoming disunited or losing balance, then maintaining counter canter in big serpentine loops (say, three) in the long arena, in half 20m circles and in corners, is unlikely to be a problem. Remember not to ride counter canter too deep into corners to begin with as you'll unbalance the horse and he'll either break from the canter, or lose the canter quality by taking short, stiff strides, or he'll swing his quarters out in order to cope.

The quality of the canter, true or counter, needs to be uppermost in the rider's mind because it is the maintenance of quality that is important, and this is easily lost. So what are the qualities of a good canter? Impulsion and engagement, a clear three-beat rhythm, a clear moment of suspension, suppleness in the body and elasticity in the steps, straightness, and a forward, uphill tendency. Further, the horse should already know how to shorten and lengthen the stride within the canter without resistance or tension, so the rider can set him up for whatever is to come.

SIMPLE CHANGES

A simple change is a change of pace from canter to walk to canter, without any intervening trot strides up or down. However, these are introduced in the earlier tests, and to start with, a couple (literally) of progressive trot strides into walk are allowed. However, the upward transition from walk to canter should be direct. These changes are all about the preparation, or set-up, of the movement in conjunction with efficient half-halts, and without losing the fluency of the overall movement.

They can be asked for almost anywhere in the arena: on the centreline in the middle of two half 10m circles on the BXE line, on the long side, on the diagonal line, or in serpentines, and all involve a change of canter lead. The aid from canter to walk should be given as a half-halt on the inside rein at the point when the horse is taking weight behind at the beginning of a canter stride – when the hindlegs are on the ground and are, actually, already in the walk sequence. The outside rein is there for the collection of the horse into shorter canter steps before the simple change, and a half-halt on the inside rein will interrupt the flow of the canter.

The key to achieving this change is to apply the aids at just the right moment, and then the horse should stay in balance and find the walk steps and the subsequent depart into canter very easy.

Shoulder-fore positioning can be very helpful in keeping the horse straight in the canter, but it is important to change the bend in the walk phase so that he is bent correctly for the new canter strike-off.

Done as above, the simple change can be simple; done at the wrong moment, or with aids that the horse finds confusing and doesn't understand, it's far from simple.

FLYING CHANGES

Very often an inexperienced horse will offer a flying change when he finds himself off balance. This is a good thing, as any natural talent should be nurtured. However, this doesn't mean that you should rely on this. Rather, you allow several steps of the new canter, bring the horse back to trot, and then ask for a transition into canter. However thrilling it is to discover that your horse can do flying changes, for everyone's future success it does need to be your decision and not his! What you must not do is make him feel bad for having done a change.

Flying changes can be trained because the horse naturally has a moment of suspension between each three-beat stride, which is when he can literally change his legs in the air. However, we're not suggesting that you give your aid at that moment. Most of us simply prepare our aids and give them to the horse so that, by practice and repetition, he knows that we'd like him to change and he does it at the next possible moment. If you are able to be more precise, then give the aid to change when the leading foreleg comes forward as the last step of the canter stride.

However, the following are basic requirements: first and foremost, the quality of the canter has to be good enough (off the forehand and with enough 'jump') to allow him to change; second, he needs to change the flexion easily and willingly; third, he needs to be straight and able to do simple changes left and right with ease; fourth, he has to totally understand, wait for and obey left and right canter aids; and fifth, he needs to be on the aids. So you can see why the exercises already mentioned do much to bring the horse to the point where flying changes can be introduced.

The rider is very important when introducing flying changes; ideally, it's good to learn them on a horse that has already has been trained, so that the rider can get a good 'feel' of what's necessary. However, if all the above advice has been put into practice, the rider should also be ready to attempt a change.

How To Do It

Most horses – though not all, of course – change more easily from right to left, so this is the exception to our rule of explaining everything on the left rein. The aids for a change from right canter to left canter, via a flying change, are as follows:

- Left seatbone weighted and left hip forwards (lead with your hip – change from right canter position into left canter position)
- Slight flexion left at the poll and jaw
- Half-halt on the right (outside) rein
- Right leg back
- Left leg on the girth
- Keep the contact on the right rein, give the left rein slightly forwards

Give all these aids as simultaneously as you can, and your horse should change. Don't look down to check, as that changes your balance, which doesn't help your horse; rather, make sure there's someone there who can tell you if the change worked.

The following exercises will help this process along. They work best in the long arena where there is more room for manoeuvre, but all can be adapted for the short arena without much effort.

In right canter, take a short diagonal from the quarter marker to the middle marker; at the three-quarter line, trot, leg yield to the track, straighten, shoulder-fore and canter left. Do this until it flows very well and you can make the transitions and the changes of bend quickly and easily. You reduce the number of trot strides until it is virtually direct, and if all has gone well, your horse is likely to anticipate the change of lead and offer it. Let him!

Alternatively, take the centreline, ride towards B or E, trot and leg yield towards the marker and on the track straighten and canter on the new lead.

Or, start a series of serpentine loops (three or five, depending on the size of the arena): as you cross the first centreline make a simple change; over the next centreline, another simple change and so on; till you get the point where again, the horse anticipates a change coming up and you can ask for a flying change.

Another exercise on the serpentine loops is as follows: pick up right canter, and as you come to the centreline the first time, put your horse into travers right, straighten and ask for a change; the second time you come to the centreline put your horse into travers left, straighten and ask for a change; and continue like this. This exercise works because you are displacing the quarters and making it easier for the horse to want to change because you have deliberately put him in an unbalanced position.

Yet another exercise is to take up half-pass in canter right from the centreline to the middle marker on the long side; straighten on to the track, reposition into shoulder-fore, and give the aids for left canter. Again, anticipation can be your friend. Then you can half-pass from the quarter marker on to the centre line, straighten, reposition and change.

As a test to see if you've both mastered this single flying change, come on to the long diagonal, and try a change somewhere on it (again, use right to left when you first have a go at this); however, do make sure that your horse stays straight on the line.

- We want to emphasize here the importance of your horse being in both reins, straight, on the aids, and in particular, that the rider can soften the new inside rein so that the horse can, so to speak, change 'into' it.

AVOIDING TENSION

Lots of horses become anxious when learning changes and try to run away, or explode, while doing this work. In this case, do something else, and return to it later. For this reason, it can be a good idea to concentrate on changes one way only until they are totally established (and this can take quite a long time until the horse is confident and relaxed), so obviously, you use the horse's natural propensity to change the way that he finds easiest.

One exercise that we're not so keen on, because in our experience it can be difficult to control the quarters, is going from one 20m circle (or half circle) to another, with a change over the centreline. It is often used, but we find that horses easily learn to swing the quarters unless great care is taken to make sure they are straight for several strides before the new lead. If horses learn to swing their quarters whilst doing changes, it can be really difficult to correct this, and the sequence changes become correspondingly more difficult to achieve correctly.

Too much emphasis on changing the bend can mean that the rider forgets the other important aspects of riding a change, such as the canter quality, the straightness, the forward tendency, and the freedom of the new inside shoulder. Too much bend is more of a problem than too little, as it takes too long for the horse to move his quarters over out of the way to change through from behind. Slowing right down in an attempt to collect the horse can also be counter-productive, as there won't be enough impulsion from behind for the horse to jump through energetically.

Actually, keeping the horse straight into both reins, with a consistent feel on each rein, is probably one of the most important considerations before a change. If the horse is inclined to want to jump to one side – for example, when the rider wants to set up a right-to-left change and the horse wants to fall out through the right shoulder (a right-handed horse) – the rider really needs to make sure that the horse can't do that, and it can be useful to use the whip to reinforce the change aid, as in 'do it now', together with the release of the new inside rein.

With a sensitive horse, the rider needs to be equally sensitive, particularly with the spur, as such a horse is likely to kick out against it and as a result lose the sequence of the footfall, with the result that both horse and rider will be likely to lose concentration. A less sensitive horse can be helped to 'jump through' with the judicious use of a whip on the same side as the rider's new outside leg. Sometimes it can be better to activate the inside hindleg with a tap of the whip before the change so as not to disturb the actual change.

Undoubtedly you've seen all sorts of gymnastic gyrations that various riders seem to use, throwing themselves forwards and/or coming right out of the saddle, in conjunction with an outside leg which almost reaches the horse's tail! And if the horse is really unlucky, that same rider will hook him in the teeth at just the moment he needs to have the freedom to do the change. The more violent the aids, the less harmony there will be between horse and rider, and the rougher or more incorrect the changes are likely to be. The horse needs the rider to sit quiet, in a correct position, to use clear simultaneous aids, and not interfere too much.

With flying changes, the horse should change because of the rider's definite, but subtle aids. The rider's feel is a very important element in riding flying changes and, for that, the rider needs to be in the saddle – it isn't the rider who is supposed to do the flying!

SEQUENCE CHANGES

When everything as described above is in place, the rider could attempt a series of changes on the long sides of the arena without worrying about counting the strides between the changes. You probably need to come in off the track on to the quarter line to give the horse room to change without crashing into, or backing off, the arena side. What is important is the straightness and the quality of the canter, and that the horse stays relaxed in his mind, in balance, and waits for the aids.

● By the quality of the canter, we mean that the canter should have the same rhythm, tempo, balance, cadence and jump, before, during and after each change.

Don't be too obsessed with the horse's outline as long as he stays on the aids, and don't worry if the changes aren't always clean and that he doesn't always respond as quickly as you'd like him to. All this comes with time, so give him the time to deal with these new demands, and be understanding and sympathetic to his anxieties. It's really important that he should remain 'happy' about the changes, as worry and stress will set back the establishment of the changes by a long way. Practice does make perfect, but it can also be good to stop on a good note – there's always another day.

At this stage, changes on the diagonal can be counter-productive because it's too easy for the straightness to suffer as there's no track, or arena fence, to help with this. Any tension that results from the changes can mean that every time the horse comes on to the diagonal, he becomes anxious, and starts changing all over the place! If you must do them, it's a very good idea to ride diagonals without any changes on a regular basis to reduce tension and make sure your horse waits for your aids.

  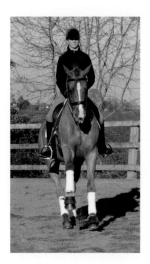 

Changes on the diagonal out of the corner on the right rein.

Now we start to count. Although horses are really quite bright and can certainly anticipate what we might want, as far as we know they can't actually count – however, they do, of course, react to any change of position you might make. It really does matter that your horse only changes when you ask him to do so.

Counting the Canter Strides

At this stage you need to learn to count each canter stride, so a good plan is to canter round the arena counting the strides without doing any changes at all. When you can confidently count canter strides, think about what is required from Prix St Georges (PSG) up: at that level, the requirements are for a change every fourth stride, five in total, and then a change every three strides, again five in total. At higher levels the requirements are for a change every two strides, and ultimately, one-time changes. (The shorthand terms are '4s', '3s', '2s' and '1s'.)

There are two common methods of counting, starting with four-time changes; the first version is:

One, two, three, four, change; *two*, two, three, four, change; *three*, two, three, four, change; *four*, two, three, four, change; *five*.

The change aid is given as the fourth stride takes place. The second version of counting is:

One, two, three, and, change; *two*, two, three, and, change; and so on.

All that has happened here is that 'and' is substituted for 'four'; the change aid is then given on the 'and'. For '3s' or '2s', reduce the numbers accordingly.

● Counting is good, but you do need to remember to give the aids, while keeping the fluency and straightness of the canter as well!

Concentrate on your horse and his way of going as your first concern; counting is difficult, and it takes much practice and good co-ordination. As we said earlier, this is where some space is good, either a large arena or a field.

When things are going smoothly on the long sides, you can vary the number of sequence changes you ask for – sometimes two '4s' or '3s', sometimes three, occasionally five – so that the horse continues to listen to what you want. When this goes well, it's probably safe to use the diagonal line from time to time.

Divide the diagonal line into three sections mentally, and aim to do two changes before X, one over X, and two after X (for PSG). This gives you time to set the horse up before the changes, and time to deal with any transition and/or the corner after you've finished the changes – always remembering that the last change must be on the diagonal line and not on the track at the quarter marker. (This also applies in Advanced Medium, where you go in medium or extended canter across the diagonal, then collect and change before the quarter marker, and not when you're safely back on the track, where the change would be easier to make. Also, in the canter across the diagonal, keep your canter aids very clear and in place, and your preparation to collect similarly clear, and only then give the aids to change – otherwise you're likely to have the extension, the collection and the change all in one big muddled mess!)

Good changes are those ridden forwards, in an even rhythm and cadenced tempo, with the horse jumping cleanly through from behind, staying straight, on the aids, and with as much expression as the quality of the canter allows.

We have not discussed one-time changes because if all the above is in place, it's just a question of very quick minimal aids. Such changes are really a different movement, since

Right *Left* *Right*

Tempi changes.

Left *Right*

you don't actually canter left or right during the changes because the horse is changing all the time – the pictures show this quite clearly.

ZIG-ZAGS (COUNTER CHANGES OF HAND)

Counter changes of hand (otherwise known as zig-zags) come next. These start simply enough with just one zig and zag, but get more complex the higher up the levels you go.

There are basically three challenges associated with canter zig-zags: half-passes are combined with the flying changes; there is no wall to help you; and you must be able to count, accurately, the number of strides between each half-pass, incorporating the last stride of the 'old' canter into the first stride of the 'new' canter lead whilst changing direction smoothly and without hesitation. Not forgetting the quality of the canter, the straightness of the changes, and a clear change of bend into the new half-pass upon each change of direction!

In this movement, the margin between success and error is quite narrow, and very dependent on the correctness of the training and the willingness of your horse to stay in front of your leg and wait for your aids. In addition, as most horses go much more easily to one side than to the other, you can end up with the quarters swinging wildly out of control and the zig-zag rather uneven.

At the beginning it will take up most people's concentration and effort to do one zig from the centreline from half-marker to the quarterline in the small arena, or to X in the big arena, with a zag back to where you came from, only further down. The school wall gives some help in stopping the flow of the quarters and enables you to straighten your horse and ask for the change; your horse will quite quickly start to

expect a change aid, but it is important that he allows you to straighten him, and waits for the change aid.

It really matters that the canter half-pass with the correct bend, and the flying change, are both totally established so there is no problem with either movement before you start these counter changes of hand. Then you can go for zig, zag, zig, without worrying about any particular counting accuracy, while keeping the forwardness, the balance and the clear changes of bend in the half-pass, with clean flying changes. Fit them in where you can, with quality and correctness at the forefront of your mind.

In a test situation, it's important to analyse where the zig-zags need to start and finish, mathematically, so that there is time and room to complete the movement, without rushing or having to pull and push. A few straight strides on the centreline after the zig-zags are always required, so you have to factor those in as well. So the sooner the zig-zag is started, the more likely it is that you'll complete the whole thing without running out of arena.

The change itself will count as a stride, so the counting needs to be adapted to accommodate this. So with four strides of half-pass left, the aid would need to be given one stride earlier than with straightforward changes so that the landing of the change is the first stride of the next sequence of strides.

Counter change of hand is a movement which could easily cause your horse to lose confidence, so it pays dividends to take the learning process slowly and carefully, concentrating on quality and forwardness.

- It is probably true to say that this is often one of the less elegantly ridden movements that one sees – but it doesn't have to be like that!

15 Test Riding and Arena Craft

Experience is what you get right after you need it.

(Unknown)

Dressage is the French term for training. It has often come to mean learning the movements to get through a test. Without understanding the concept, or the point of the movements and what they are supposed to achieve in terms of training the horse, test riding is not of much value.

In our view, dressage means maximizing the quality of the horse's natural paces combined with correct training, and the excellent communication that should come with that, so that the horse can be shown off to the best possible advantage and thus be a pleasure to ride and to judge. Then test riding comes into its own as a way of checking your progression and correctness against an established set of criteria.

Up to Medium level, virtually any horse can get through a test. In fact, that is often what a judge is confronted with – a combination just

Aachen's main arena at night – scary or what?! The spectator capacity is plus/minus 50,000.

going through the motions, rather than the presentation of a well ridden and trained horse going easily within himself in harmony with the rider. Actually, some naturally talented horses get much further than this, and are presented in competition at levels way beyond the correctness of their basic work.

Training horses takes time, patience and knowledge. The phrase 'I've got time' should be tattooed on every dressage rider's forehead! Alois Podhajsky wisely said in one of his books that 'We can achieve the highest goals in the art of riding only when we increase our demands on the horse in a systematic manner', meaning 'Take the time it takes'. In actual fact the horse dictates to a large extent the time it takes to establish the work before moving on, rather than the ambitions of the rider.

All athletes, riders and horses, need time to build up their mental and physical abilities in a progressive manner; time to gain experience; time and patience to train a horse; time to keep the horse mentally and physically fit enough to continue to work and improve over the years. Without these elements, what is produced really isn't 'dressage'. Some horses struggle with the work, and wishing your horse could do something, regardless of temperament, conformation or lack of training, sadly doesn't make it so. Simply wanting to be a ballet dancer, but having a challenging conformation, such as short legs and huge feet, doesn't make that person a ballet dancer: it makes him or her a frustrated and miserable dancer. He or she could, of course, easily be a very talented writer, gardener or singer, for instance. Horses for courses!

THE BASICS

We do appreciate that not everyone wants, or needs, to ride dressage tests. Not everyone is competitive, and many people find the whole idea of riding in public rather alarming.

Experience for the Horse

Some horses find the atmosphere and the hustle and bustle of competitions equally alarming, but in general this can be overcome by continued exposure to such places. What can work quite well is to take your young or inexperienced horse out to some local shows, preferably with a more established horse who takes such outings in his stride. The idea is not to add the pressure of competition to visiting new places, but just to let the horse see, hear and feel what's going on. In-hand showing as a youngster can be most useful, if it's appropriate to your circumstances and the horse is a candidate for such classes. Otherwise, some low key showing under saddle is another useful tool.

Even if you have no intention of competing, it's still very helpful to have a horse that is worldly wise and calm; however, this always means that they must be given the experience of being exposed to various situations.

Experience for the Rider

If you are new to competition yourself, another idea is to go along to a dressage competition to watch and learn. Perhaps offer your services to the organizer as a helper – anything, really, that prepares you for what's to come and adds to the chances of your first competition being a good experience. If you sit in or write for a judge, you will gain a different perspective that will hold you in good stead for your competition riding, and give you an appreciation of the 'other side of the fence', so to speak.

Whether or not you are going to compete at affiliated competitions (that is, at an official BD one), it is advisable to obtain a rule book (as a member you should receive one automatically) so that you know the ins and outs of dressage competition. Most unaffiliated competitions keep more or less to BD's rules, and most judges at such events have some working knowledge of the way in which BD expects competitions to be judged; in fact unaffiliated competitions quite often use BD-trained judges.

Knowing the Rules

There are a great many rules; ignorance of them is not an excuse, and is not accepted as a reason for transgressing. You, as the rider, are totally responsible for knowing the rules and adhering to them (not the trainer, the caller, the competition organizer, your mum and definitely not your horse!). Furthermore the rules change slightly – whether amended, removed or added to – each year. New tests are added annually. In the competition schedules laid out in *British Dressage* magazine, the relevant tests are clearly shown: for example Preliminary 15 (2008), Advanced Medium 94 (2002) or Elementary 45 (2010). These schedules also contain venue-specific information, e.g. where they are located and any special rules (not all venues allow dogs on site, for example). Make sure you have the most up-to-date information – it's your responsibility.

Controlling the Controllable

A perceived wisdom is that it's sensible to choose a level of competition that's at least one, and possibly two, levels below that at which you work at home. Then you, and your horse, should find the work well within your scope, even allowing for tensions and worries about that first expedition. A snippet of psychology is that you should focus on controlling the controllable, which would be you, your horse, your training, your transport, your tack and clothing, learning the test/s, your warm-up. Don't dwell on those things you can't control, such as the weather, the judging, the other competitors – acknowledge them all, but then concentrate on

your 'bubble'. Allowing yourself to become distracted by such uncontrollables can make you anxious to no avail. Don't go there!

Take a Companion

If at all possible, take someone with you for moral and actual support and help. This can take a lot of the strain off any competitor, never mind a first-timer. It helps if they know your temperament and are good at handling your horse, but the latter is not necessary, and there are lots of things a non-horsey companion can do to make your life easier – hold your jacket, check on the dog in the lorry, get you a coffee, even keep well-wishers at bay!

At local dressage competitions it is generally possible to have a caller or commander, who shouts out the instructions on the dressage sheet so that you don't have to rely on your memory, which very often goes blank at just the wrong moment. This should not be a substitute for knowing the test: it's an *aide memoire* and a large degree of moral support. However, it's more useful if the caller and you have had some practice together so that you're both on the same wavelength – the instructions need to be given enough in advance so you know what's coming next, but not so far in advance that you forget. Instructions aren't much use if you've already passed the necessary marker or are on the wrong line altogether. Also, since the caller is not allowed to deviate from the written word (other than to shorten it), or to repeat himself, it's not quite as easy as it may sound to be a caller. A well projected clear voice is necessary as often the tests are outside, sometimes in adverse weather conditions – or perhaps the caller is in competition with callers of other tests in other arenas.

● Using your voice during a test is not allowed and you'll lose marks; it doesn't matter whether you are clicking at your horse, or speaking to your caller, or to anyone else: don't do it!

At the Competition

So you've done your preparation; your horse knows something about the outside world; and you've turned up at the event. Go straight to the secretary's office, declare (tell them you're there), and find out if the competition is running to time; find the locations of the loo, the warm-up and test-riding arenas, and whether or not there is a steward (if not, you'll have to keep an eye on the time for yourself) – all so that you're comfortable with your surroundings and can give yourself the necessary time to get yourself ready and prepared.

Dressage tests are divided into time slots, and when you phone for your time (the details for this will be in the schedule), you can work back from that to give yourself enough time to drive to the venue, find out what you need to know when you get there, tack up and unload your horse, warm him up and be ready to compete at your designated time. (If you can't compete for any reason, please let the organizer know: it's just polite, and at affiliated competitions a 'no show' is marked down on the results sheets that go into the BD office, and you could find yourself receiving a reprimand.)

You will also be allocated a number to put on the bridle or the saddle cloth so that you can be identified by the steward, if there is one, and definitely by the judge – this is really quite important, as judges are not clairvoyant and do need to know who you are. (On a welfare note, your number would also be useful in identifying you or your horse if either were involved in an incident or accident, and in fact it's in the BD rule book that competitors should have their number visible at all times when exercising or riding.) You should also always wear a hat or helmet when mounted at a competition, whether or not you are actually competing.

THE WARM-UP

Test riding and arena craft start with the warm-up, and this phase is often the one where tests are won and lost. At official BD competitions the warm-up is generally in a surfaced arena, and there will be a number of other riders in there with you. There are some basic rules for safety and convenience, the foremost of which is that you should ride 'left hand to left hand'. Probably in equal second come 'give way to a faster pace' and 'don't walk or halt on the track'. Giving way to lateral work, counter canter and extensions are other 'rules' but these are less well known and kept.

If you want to adjust your girth, your clothing or have your horse's rugs, boots or bandages adjusted or removed, please do not do this on the track, or on a diagonal. Riding round the track in pairs talking to each other, or using your mobile, is not behaviour which will endear you to other competitors. Another is wielding your long dressage whip like a weapon, catching riders or horses as they go past.

Whilst keeping all this in mind, remember that your warm-up is as important as anyone else's, and being ridden off by someone less considerate, or someone who thinks they own the arena, can be intimidating: you can find yourself riding a very small circle in the middle of the arena to keep out of everyone else's way. Don't let this happen to you, however; you have a voice and you might need to use it – but politely. Also make sure that you are not causing someone else a problem. If you are going faster than someone else, either turn away, give them plenty of room, or say 'Track, please' in the hope that they will turn off the track. Bear in mind that some horses don't like another one coming up fast behind them, or close in, or coming straight at them. Make sure you are not the one who transgresses whilst keeping your own agenda firmly in your mind.

These days many people ride stallions and, in the main, they behave very well – but if they do start playing up, get out of the way and stay out of the way! And if you have a mare in season, stay alert. Be considerate; some people will be on youngsters, or older horses that haven't been out much and/or are spooky, or on something that spends most of the time spinning round or standing on two legs; so watch out and make sure you don't ride too close, or cause them trouble.

In the hunting field, a discreet green ribbon on the top of the tail means that the horse is 'inexperienced' or 'novice'; a red ribbon means 'this horse might kick' or even 'this horse will kick', and some dressage riders do use ribbons in this way – so take note. (At the end of BD Rule 58, it states 'Stallions may be identified by the rider wearing a yellow cross band whilst working in.' Neither of us has ever seen this, but we have definitely seen the red and green ribbons.)

It is useful to have an established warm-up programme with which both you and your horse are familiar. Time it at home so you know when your horse is ready for the test, but give yourself a bit more time to deal with any tension or problems that surface in a competition atmosphere. And remember that anything you and your horse haven't learnt at home won't suddenly, magically, come right at the competition.

● Schooling at home and preparing your horse for a competition are not the same thing.

At home you might well work on the things your horse is not so good at, as well as those things he can do. At a competition, you are there to show how good you both are, so you maximize the good things and do the best you can with the weaker movements. Taking risks in the competition arena goes with the territory, but make them calculated risks.

Don't make the mistake of thinking that riding test movements at home is enough: they need to be strung together, because in a test it is unbelievable just how fast things come up, and there's no time for thinking 'Where am I?' and 'What should I do now?' This is related to confidence: if you freeze on entering the arena, your horse doesn't have much choice but to join you in the freeze. He needs you to be his confident herd leader as he has just left the warm-up arena where his equine compatriots are, and is now on his own – and he needs you to tell him that everything's fine and that he should just concentrate on you.

● Test riding is a skill that needs to be understood and practised.

KNOW THE TEST

Knowing the test might sound so obvious as to be insulting, but what we mean is that not only should you know what to do, and when, but also *why* one movement follows another, and the logic behind the sequences.

Tests are, believe it or not, written with the aim of showing off the horse's training and paces in a logical pattern to bring out the best performance. Tests set training questions, and correct answers are rewarded with good marks, but if you don't know what you're doing and why, then the test will seem to be a random mix of movements with no discernible point, and can be more difficult to learn and perform as a result.

So what is the point of a 10m circle at the quarter marker before a shoulder-in? Done well, the circle gives you the bend and control of the shoulders; it should also give you the opportunity to adjust the energy level and increase the activity of the hindlegs. And what is the point of doing a medium trot across the diagonal after a corner? Ridden properly, the corner gives you the chance to develop the same qualities mentioned above so that the horse has enough impulsion to produce the trot you have asked for.

LEARNING THE TEST

Some people learn the test by heart just by reading the sheet; others practise on foot (perhaps on a rectangular rug at home); others ride the test/s in walk whilst reciting the test to themselves; others visualize riding the test until they are 'foot' perfect. There are lots of aids available these days to help with test riding: wipe-clean boards with all the markers on them on which you can draw; laminated diagrams of the various movements in each test; DVDs of the various tests to watch; and audio CDs to which you can listen. What you use will reflect your particular style of learning.

Every test starts and finishes with a centreline, ridden in trot or canter, depending upon the level of the test; some have a halt at the beginning (at X); some have a few steps of walk before the final salute; and all have a halt and salute at X or G at the end of the test.

At the lower levels it's perfectly acceptable to be progressive in your transitions, so for instance you could do two walk strides into halt, rather than trot down the centre line and make an abrupt, unbalanced halt. Rising trot to halt (or walk) is very difficult to do successfully, and more often than not, you end up pulling at the horse to stop. Doing something at the last moment always looks like it – and you'll be marked accordingly.

The better balanced the halt, the more likely it is that the horse will stay on the aids and be ready to move off when asked; again, a couple of strides of walk before the trot are allowed – but don't push your luck, because any more than that suggests your horse isn't listening.

RIDE YOUR CORNERS

Ride corners as if you are riding between two curved walls, and prepare early enough that your horse bends correctly on the curved line; Hubertus Schmidt recommends starting the

preparation for a corner at least 10m beforehand.

When a turn is required, ride through 90 degrees – actually it's very little different from a correctly ridden corner. Ride straight lines on the track unless otherwise directed or a curved line is requested. Commence each movement at the designated marker: according to the FEI this should be when your shoulder is at the marker, but this requires extreme precision, so it's perhaps a bit easier to line up with your outside knee (which should be pretty much in line with your shoulder anyway); and come off the track at the marker if the movement requires it.

CIRCLES

Be sure that you make your circles totally circular! There should be no straight lines or angles in a circle at any point from start to finish. Visually, it can be useful to imagine a diamond shape in the arena surface; ride to each tangent point with just enough curve to accommodate the size of the circle. 'Tangent' is a geometric term: if you can imagine putting a circle inside a square, the tangent points are where the two figures touch, and from there you can draw an imaginary diamond shape – so as the drawing on page 144 shows, a diamond inside a circle inside a square. This way you stand a chance of

Corner – again!

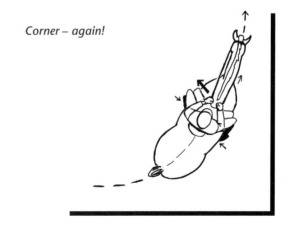

making the four quarters of the circle the same size – which, be assured, is quite unusual!

The next drawing shows circle sizes: in the short arena, 6m, 8m and 10m voltes (small circles) are possible at every marker, and 15m and 20m circles at A, E, C, B. In the long arena, the small circles can be ridden at every marker, and 15m and 20m circles at V, S, R and P as well as at A, E, C and B.

If you ride a smaller circle than is required, you are unnecessarily increasing the difficulty of the movement for you and your horse (and you don't get bonus marks!); conversely, if you ride a bigger circle than is asked for you are making it easier, but you will be penalized as

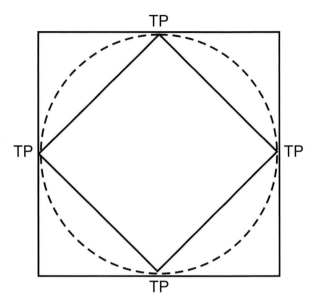

Circle – again! A diamond inside a circle inside a square; the tangent points are where the diamond's edges touch the square.

the size of the circle is prescribed to demonstrate the degree and correctness of the training, and collection, that you and your horse have in place.

A circle requires that the horse comes off the track at the marker – not a couple of strides after it, as it can't be a circle if you start with straight strides – and then describes the required diameter, returning to the original marker at the end of the circle. The rider should then ride the following corner, at A or C, or use the circle as the preparation for the next movement.

Sometimes there is a transition at a marker, and a requirement for a circle at the same marker. In this event you need to make the transition and also come off the track at exactly the same time.

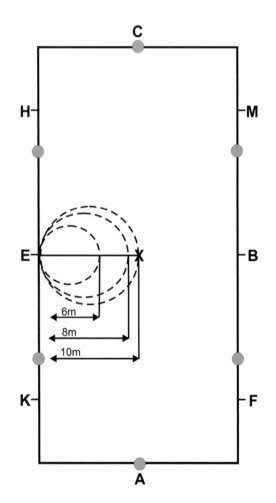

Lots of circles!

DIAGONAL LINES/ CHANGING THE REIN

Diagonal lines can be long or short: examples

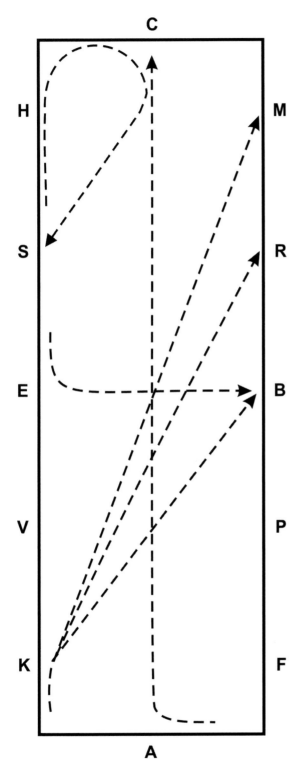

C

H

S

E

V

K

A

M

R

B

P

F

Diagonals and changes of rein.

are HXF in both arenas, KB in both arenas, RXV and HIB in the long arena, and so on, as shown in the diagram. They are straight lines, but often ridden from a quarter marker, or off a bent line, and one of the things that can happen is that the rider doesn't straighten the horse on to the line. If an extension is required on the diagonal line, or flying changes, this often means that the horse struggles with the balance and loses considerable power because he isn't correctly aligned and straight before the movement starts, and he drifts through his outside shoulder off the line or swings his quarters.

Such lines, together with half-circles back to the track and turns off the centreline or across the arena, are often used to effect a change of rein.

THE MATHEMATICS OF THE ARENA

Know the mathematics of the arena so that you are accurate, and the movements are correctly sized and/or started and finished where they should be. Whilst accuracy and precision are more than desirable, there's some leeway at the lower levels, as the way of going and fluency are more important than total accuracy.

Be sure that you are familiar with the markers. There seems to be little in the way of logic about the letters used; why they are where they are, and what they are, are lost in the mists of time – and anyway, who cares!

With A at the halfway point (middle) of the top short side, and going clockwise, the short arena (20 × 40m) markers are:

A, K, E, H, C, M, B, F
(K, H, M, F are quarter markers, and E and B are half markers on the long sides of the arena)
Down the centre line the letters used are: D (between K and F); X (between E and B); and G (between H and M)

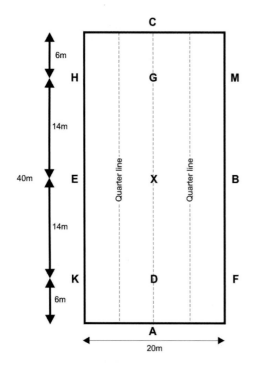

Arenas: the long arena is 20 × 60m, the short arena is 20 × 40m.

In the long arena (20 × 60m), the markers are:

A, K, V, E, S, H, C, M, R, B, P, F
Down the centre line, the extra letters to those used in the short arena are: L (between V and P) and I (between S and R)

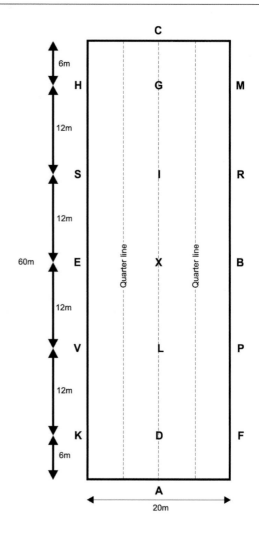

Learn them so well that you don't ever have to think about them again, and then it won't matter if the arena you'll be riding in faces the other way from the one you are used to.

Then you need to do some maths. All arenas are 20m wide, so it follows that the centre line is 10m from each side, and each side is divisible again into two lots of 5m, with one quarterline on each side of the centreline. Arenas come in only two lengths, 40m and 60m, with markers (*see* above) down both long sides, and one marker on each short side, A and C. As the diagram shows, the short arena is 40m long, so from B and E there is 20m on each side to the

corner. It is always 6m from the corner of the arena to the first quarter marker, which leaves 14m between each quarter marker and the half marker: therefore down each long side you have 6 + 14 + 14 + 6 = 40m.

The long arena is 60m long, so B and E are at 30m from the corners. The quarter markers are still in the same places (6m from the corners). V, S, R and P are 12m from the respective quarter markers, and also 12m from the half markers, so down each side you have 6 + 12 + 12 + 12 + 12 + 6 = 60m.

Loops and serpentines are required in several tests. One aspect of serpentines is that the loops should all be of equal size.

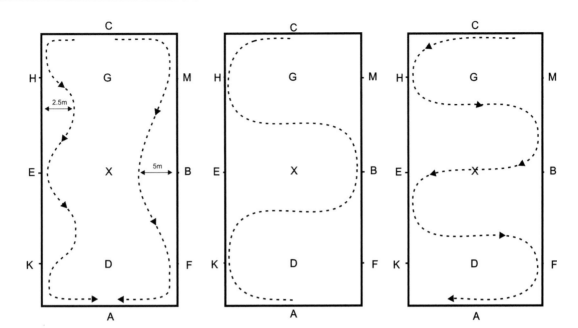

Circles were discussed earlier; they were illustrated in the short arena, but the diagrams are equally applicable to the long arena, with some mathematical adjustments.

DRESSAGE JUDGES

The master judge, often the only one, sits at C. At a bigger competition you might find two more judges sitting on each long side of the arena, perhaps at M and H, or B and E, or B and M, or other variations on a theme. At championships there are often five judges, and always at international competitions, the two 'extra' ones sitting at E and B. The number of judges is currently under review, pending an FEI decision. Judges can be in a car, at a table, on a raised platform, or in a purpose-made judging box; all of these tend to cause horses to back off and spook, so it can be a good idea to practise riding towards such horrors beforehand.

Judges are often much maligned, but it is all too easy to blame the judge for the marks you receive. Judges are human, and they want to give good marks (in spite of what you might

ABOVE: Four-loop serpentine, three-loop serpentine, and single and double loops.

RIGHT: A five-loop serpentine in the long arena.

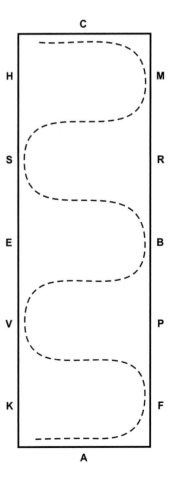

have heard), but they can't do that if the competitor they are judging falls short of the criteria by which they have to judge. In the UK, British Dressage judges at all levels are volunteers who receive only travel money for doing their job; they are passionate about dressage, and at their own cost have undergone an extensive educational training programme in order to be qualified to sit in that car or box. They have only a few seconds to respond to what the competitor does in each of the movements – probably twenty or more in most tests – during which time they have to evaluate the adherence to the Scales of Training, the FEI definitions of the movements, the rider's skill, the actual execution of the movements, and the horse's way of going, as well as giving a mark for each movement, and often a remark as well.

Each movement is marked out of 10 (excellent) down to 0 (not performed). Often there is more than one element to each marked movement, which leads to a compromise mark because the competitor did a really good halt, say, but the rein-back was crooked or resistant, and/or the move-off was reluctant – taking the potentially high mark down to something less desirable, depending on what happened. Furthermore judges definitely cannot mark what you don't do – so if you are asked to show 'medium trot strides' or 'trot, two strides of walk, and trot', you do need to attempt it, and also try to fulfil all the criteria for the movement.

In short, riders, judges and trainers should all be working along the same lines, to the same objectives. If you feel that this doesn't appear to be the case, then start some dialogue. Approached in a civilized fashion, most judges would be glad to discuss what you did and what they saw (which is not always the same thing), although they would probably need to see your sheet to remind themselves what had happened. Try it, if you feel you have issues.

RIDING THE TEST

At the time of writing, the following are some of the rules used in British dressage; they might not be relevant, or worded similarly, elsewhere in the world; they can, and do, change as dressage evolves.

There is a rule – 'the 45-second rule' – that says you should enter the arena to start your test within 45 seconds of the signal that the judge is ready for you. The penalty for exceeding this limit is subject to some change, so check your rule book. Quite often, ignoring this rule causes classes to run late (multiply just one extra minute per competitor in a class of thirty, and it'll be half an hour late finishing, not to mention messing up everyone's carefully planned warm-up sessions). If you ride round the whole of a long arena after the signal has gone, you will be in breach of this rule because it takes longer than that to get round (unless you gallop!). So turn back on yourself and get started! Check whether you have to ride round the outside of the arena (this is usual) or whether you can ride inside. Ask the organizer or steward.

● There is no 'right' to ride round the arena once, twice, or at all – you should be ready to start your test as soon as you arrive at the arena, if necessary.

Be alert for the signal (usually a bell or a horn), especially if there are several arenas being used at the same time. Try to be calm enough to recognize that sound, so that if you hear a similar sound during your test, only stop if you've gone wrong, or if you are sure it's your judge who is signalling. Unfortunately the onus is on you: if you stop because you thought the signal was for you, and it wasn't, the judge might penalize you for stopping in mid-movement.

Another rule you need to know is that you must not ride around the edge of, or in, the

Halt, salute. On the aids, attentive and a square halt: Kyra Kyrklund (Finland) and Max.

arena if the judge is not in place, regardless of what any steward might have told you. It's a hard lesson to learn, as transgressing can lead to elimination. Check also whether you are allowed to carry a whip. Rules about this vary; for example, 'no whips' is the rule at championships.

The rules described above apply at all levels, although it is to be hoped that judges judging lower level classes would apply some common sense and consideration for inexperienced riders, and simply explain where they had gone wrong without penalizing them. But don't count on it – it's your responsibility to know the rules and to abide by them.

Entry and Salute

● Your entry is your big moment to impress the judge and make him or her sit up and take extra note of your brilliance – you only get one go at a first impression! Be sure to make your entry on the horse's more

supple side so that the turn on to the centreline is as accurate as possible.

Fix your eyes on C where the judge sits, and ride positively forwards. If there's a halt at X at the beginning of the test, remember that the salute to the judge should be made with whip and reins in one hand, so that you can salute with your free hand (this has been in the rule book for many years, so please take note). Smiling is good! The salute is best done simply with a nod of the head; some people do a very fancy salute, rather like that of a Cavalier with a plumed hat, but this is unnecessary and it is harder to keep your horse on the bit, still and attentive whilst doing it. Don't make the halt too brief or too prolonged; a count of six works well. All this applies equally at the end of the test.

Make the Most of your Performance

Watch the top riders and see how their tests

flow. They use the whole arena to the best advantage so that the movements are prepared without losing the quality of the paces or the fluency of the performance. They don't 'give away' any marks for inaccuracy, and they don't generally forget the test. And if something does go wrong, they don't dwell on it and so mess up the next three movements.

There is some showmanship involved; a test is a performance, not a schooling session. If you must talk to your horse, do it well away from the judge; if you need to give your horse a reminding kick, try to do it without bringing attention to yourself. If your horse has gone hollow, let the rein out a bit or lower the outline momentarily while riding forwards, and see if you can retrieve things in a subtle manner.

If you are having a really horrible time, try to deal with the problems without contravening any welfare issues, and make the best of it. However, sometimes the only thing to do is retire – if that is your decision, stop what you're doing, put your hand up to signal your retirement, and leave the arena.

The Wrong Test

If you have learnt the wrong test, it's permissible to have a commander join you part way through the test if that'll solve the problem and there's someone immediately available, so

RISING TO THE TROT

Don't be afraid to rise to the trot mid-test if the level you're riding at allows it, especially if you feel your horse slowing down, or becoming hollow, or you are getting stiff. Going rising often refreshes the trot and gives the horse an opportunity to work with more freedom over his back, which in turn might give rise to higher marks.

that you can continue straightaway from where you went wrong. (Re-starting a test is at the judge's discretion and you'll be penalized for a first 'error of course'). If that's not possible, and if time allows, some judges will let you return to the arena at a later time and ride through the correct test 'HC' (*hors concours* – outside the competition; in other words, your test won't count in the results). However, you can't elect to go HC after you've ridden your test, other than in this situation.

Knowing the Rules

Do read the rules about repeating a movement, or circling where a circle is not required; in either case, the judge can only mark whatever you do first, so any further attempts will not be marked and you will also incur a two-penalty 'error of test'.

A final word on rules: national rules can differ from FEI rules in the detail, so always check the rules as they relate to your national governing body – and the FEI if relevant.

Moreover, the judges have the final say on the day, whatever you may think to the contrary. If you're still not happy, all governing bodies have a complaints system in place.

PRESENTATION

Test riding is a presentation as well as a performance, so it helps with the general impression if you and your horse are well turned out; it's a courtesy to the judge, the show organizers and the spectators; it should also make you feel good about yourself and your horse.

A clean saddle, bridle and saddle cloth, correctly fitted; a number put on straight; and a well fitting set of clothing for the rider (appropriate to the level – rule books have the information), clean shiny boots, and a well groomed horse, all help. This is not to say that everything needs to be new – in fact, new and unused at a competition are not as good as familiar and comfortable – but clean and tidy (including your hair under your hat) are good. The less jewellery the better, probably, so that nothing gets caught up or falls off.

To plait or not to plait: it is certainly traditional to do so, but not entirely necessary – although it's a good skill to learn, and your horse will look smart and workmanlike. If you don't plait, then the mane should be neatly pulled and brushed through, and it should lie flat on one side, traditionally the off side. If you do plait, please also plait the forelock: it has become fashionable in some quarters to leave it unplaited, but it doesn't look fashionable, it just looks as though someone has forgotten about it (at least, that's our opinion!).

If you like to stand out from the crowd by means of your own attire and that of your horse, it is worth bearing two things in mind: first, check that what you want to wear, or put on your horse, is allowed under the rules; and second, it's a good idea to 'stand out' because

The winners! This could be you on the podium!

your riding and training are up to par – otherwise, keeping things simple and discreet can be better.

The manes of some native breeds and Iberian horses are traditionally shown long and unplaited, some have particular types of plaiting, and all are perfectly acceptable, as is a well hogged mane. What is important is to be neat, tidy and clean.

There are two schools of thought about plaiting tails: those who do and those who don't. Again, it's more about good grooming, so a full tail, clean and well brushed out, looks really good, as does a well trimmed tail. Plaiting a tail is a lot of work for one or two classes, but plenty of people take the time and trouble to do so; however, it only looks good if the tail hairs at the top are long enough to be neatly incorporated into a plait – otherwise don't do it!

Above all, enjoy your ride and your day. It's amazing how well you can do with a positive attitude and view of life, something that your horse will pick up and might well emulate.

RENT A CROWD

A lot of horses react badly to the noises and sights at competitions, so to help him get used to this, ask the people on your yard, or your long-suffering family, and the occasional dog, to mill about while you are riding: this generally works well, after the horse has come to terms with his initial terror. Another idea is to use 'Rent-a-Crowd', or to record some clapping, shouting and general mayhem, and subject your horse to all of this on a regular basis until he becomes more or less immune.

These ideas take some organization, and should be introduced gradually to avoid accidents, but this sort of strategy can pay dividends when the chips are down.

16 The Saddle

No hour is wasted that is spent in the saddle.

(Winston Churchill)

A saddle that doesn't fit the horse and rider correctly can be the reason for bad behaviour, inhibited movement in front and behind, a sore back and actual lameness. Saddles should not be fashion statements, and are not intended to make up for deficiencies in riding ability.

Whenever possible, each horse should have his own saddle, and it should be checked on a regular basis for continuing good fit as the horse grows, matures, and changes shape. Although a saddle fitter is almost always a saddle seller, it's in his best interest to do the job properly, and there is a much greater understanding and more technology these days to help with the task of fitting saddle to horse, rather than horse to saddle.

- The saddle is probably the most underestimated piece of equipment used by professional and amateur riders.

In our experience this is a massive understatement, and we have therefore asked Jo Beavis of the National Saddle Centre to give us some professional input and advice. Both she and the authors have decided not to embark on a 'How to fit a saddle' section, as this doesn't seem appropriate; rather, Jo has talked about the considerations that she feels are important when thinking about saddles.

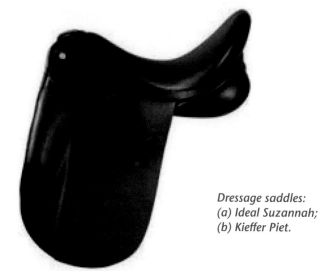

Dressage saddles:
(a) Ideal Suzannah;
(b) Kieffer Piet.

It's worth remembering that dressage is a sport requiring symmetry, which is carried out by horses and riders who are asymmetric!

The purpose of these words is to raise awareness of the contribution the saddle makes in the training of the horse. Over recent years the team supporting the modern sport horse (rider, trainer, saddler, physio, dentist, farrier, vet) has grown, and the professionals involved are increasingly aware of the importance of each one's role to the holistic wellbeing and performance of these horses.

Horses rarely present with single easily identifiable issues regarding behaviour, soundness, training and so on. It's more common for the picture to be coloured by multiple smaller problems that are harder to diagnose, and thus it's very important to be aware of the complexities and subtleties surrounding saddles, their performance and their contribution to the overall picture.

Few people are truly aware of the benefits of a saddle that fits and performs really well because it has been set up correctly for each horse and rider combination. Where little regard is paid to this link or connection between horse and rider, their performance may well be limited.

The saddle must be suitable for horse and rider, and place the rider's weight centrally in the saddle, in the optimum place for each horse, so that the horse stands a chance of remaining balanced and can use himself with maximum ease and efficiency.

Most saddles are constructed around a semi-rigid structure (the tree), the purposes of this frame being to distribute the rider's weight equally and evenly over the maximum available surface, to distribute the pressure created by girth and stirrup mountings, and, most importantly, to keep the dorsal processes of the spine free from

Jo Beavis.

downward or lateral pressure by means of a central channel or gullet.

A saddle that is correct for the rider will reduce fatigue and improve rider balance, stability and function. There are various factors relevant here: the seat width and length must be appropriate for the rider's pelvis; the seatbones need to be supported and, in the lowest part of the seat, allow the rider to remain stable and balanced; and, most importantly, maintain a neutral pelvis which is essential for flexibility in the lumbar spine.

The width of the twist of the saddle must not place too much pressure on the rider's hips, as this can result in collapse or tilting of the pelvis. Similarly, the position of the leg in the saddle must not be over-straightened as this can lead to instability and a tendency for the rider to tip forwards.

The leg position is predominantly influenced by the seat of the saddle and not the thigh blocks, as is commonly believed. A saddle that is too small doesn't allow the rider's seatbones into the lowest part of the seat and will create instability. Rather than increasing support, larger seats are inclined to create an 'armchair' effect in the rider, and this doesn't allow the rider to adopt the correct posture, either.

The size and shape of the blocks are dictated by the leg length of the rider, and their ability to remain balanced. They are also dependent on the amount of movement that the horse can demonstrate: usually the bigger the movement, the bigger the blocks required. The angle of the blocks is vital so that the thighs can maintain a dynamic and natural position behind them.

An incorrectly balanced saddle will also unbalance the rider. The most common problem is when the saddle is too low behind, which causes the rider to tilt forwards and lose the neutral position of the pelvis. This, in turn, restricts the flexibility of the lumbar spine, and therefore the rider's ability to absorb the movement of the horse. This creates a very unstable leg position as the rider tries continually to adjust his balance and position.

A correctly set-up saddle allows for the difference in the profile of the horse, from the static to the dynamic.

A saddle that bears the rider's weight equally and evenly along the longissimus dorsi (the longest, strongest muscle in the horse's back, and the one the rider sits on) does not interfere with the locomotion of the horse. This muscle is not designed to be load-bearing: it is merely a means of allowing the propulsion from the hindquarters forwards. Saddles that are incorrectly balanced impede this process, and this may lead to crookedness or tightness in the area.

It's worth noting that many horses showing loss of abdominal tone have saddle problems, because if the horse cannot stretch over the back, he can't shorten the abdominal muscles. It's fair to say that horses that are conformationally weak in the back will be limited in their potential to use themselves correctly.

There is no skeletal connection between the forelimbs of the horse and the rest of its body. The scapulae are attached by muscles and ligaments, primarily the serratus ventralis and serratus thoracis, which connect from the underside of the scapula at one end and the ribcage at the other. The placement and fit of the saddle must not affect the performance of the forelimbs of the horse by restricting the scapulae.

The saddle must be fitted with the rider 'on board'.

Regardless of the age or stage of training of a horse, placing a weight, or sitting, on the horse's ribcage immediately puts his back into extension; therefore allowances to cope with this must be made in the saddle balance.

The seat size of the saddle is also relevant to the length of the horse's ribcage, and also to the thigh length and suppleness of the rider. Too small a saddle results in weight being carried to the rear of the saddle; the rider sits behind the seat's central point, and this subtly changes the balance, making it harder for the horse to step underneath the centre of gravity and lift through the ribcage.

Few people understand that a saddle that fits a horse perfectly can still cause a significant problem, or under-performance of that horse, if the saddle is not big enough for the rider.

Saddle performance can be affected by subtle changes brought about by changes of condition, fitness, increased or decreased workload, maturity and changes to the level of training. These changes can affect the balance of the saddle – that is, where the rider's weight is; the stability of the saddle (which is of key importance for the horse to be 'connected'); the lateral stability and straightness of the saddle; and the contact area of the saddle (important for optimal weight distribution).

Preliminary findings using the most up-to-date pressure-reading systems to measure the dynamic changes of the saddle contact area in the ridden horse, and linking with computerized gait analysis, show that narrowness or squeezing of the dorsal processes on both sides, or just on one side, of the horse's spine, limits the corresponding hindleg protraction.

This gives the impression that the horse is unlevel, which reinforces the earlier statement that the saddle should not cause pressure on the dorsal processes of the spine. This latter can be caused by the gullet having insufficient clearance, or being too narrow, or by the saddle not remaining central along the horse's spine.

If the horse's conformation or way of going sends the saddle to one side, the gullet of the saddle will cross over the spine, or press on one side of it, and the horse's natural inclination will be to move away from that discomfort, thus increasing his crookedness.

No horse can be straight if the saddle and rider do not sit equally on both sides of the horse's body.

A saddle is a relatively solid and symmetrical object, and for it to remain straight on the horse's back, that back must also be similarly level and symmetrical. If a saddle that has been straight in use starts going to one side, it can be an indication of other problems. Quite frequently, saddles only go to one side on one rein, which is much harder to resolve from a saddle-fitting point of view, and in general, might well be indicative of a training issue. This is where the team influence can be most

helpful, as the saddle fit might be illustrating a problem, rather than being the cause of it. Clear identification of the underlying problem allows for a solution to be put forward, and input from all parties is essential for this to be accurate.

It is not uncommon to find that the above-mentioned problems can be influenced by the lack of development on one side of the horse, or by the horse having one noticeably larger shoulder (when viewed from behind), or one shoulder further forward than the other. The majority of horses present us with symmetry issues, and lack of saddle straightness is, therefore, a common problem that can lead to muscular soreness; however, that soreness may not be why the saddle is not sitting straight.

The saddler and trainer should, together, view the saddle, horse and rider combination from the side, the front and behind to assess the straightness, or lack of it, so that an informed diagnosis can be reached.

The position of a rider who sits in a saddle that is not straight will be negatively influenced by the fact that the pelvis will be unlevel or hitched; this leads to the shoulders being unlevel, and stiffness through the spine. This then causes an unevenness of weight distribution on the horse, with associated implications for underperformance, crookedness and loss of balance.

Since the majority of riders are not straight, either by nature or nurture, there is often a greater degree of stiffness to one side which affects the weight distribution for the horse and the straightness of the saddle; here, again, the saddle fit can be a symptom of the problem, and not the cause of it.

The saddle contact area extends from behind the scapulae to the last rib, and no pressure can be tolerated at this point as there is only muscle to support the weight.

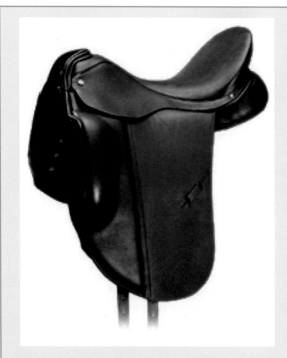

Albion SLK Ultima.

The lumbar vertebrae are different in shape from the rest of the spine and have much longer transverse processes, which can easily be damaged by the weight of the rider on a saddle that extends too far back. Such a saddle can also affect the flexibility of the horse's spine in this area, bearing in mind the lumbar spine offers some flexibility whereas the thoracic spine offers considerably less.

The shape of the horse's ribcage can also be an influential factor. Longer-legged riders sometimes struggle to get their legs on to a ribcage that narrows away under the leg, and shorter-legged riders will struggle with horses with high, well sprung ribs. The width of the seat can influence this, as a narrower seat allows a rider to have more leg against the horse's sides

and, therefore, be more effective; however, it is important not to reduce the width of the seat to the point where the seatbones are not supported, as this will lead to other issues.

A seat that is too narrow can encourage the rider to close and tighten the knee, which takes the lower leg away from the horse and causes stiffness through the upper body.

It's fair to say that no one single make of saddle will be the best solution for every horse and rider combination, despite claims to the contrary by manufacturers.

It is wise to check the relevant qualifications of the person fitting/selling you your saddle. Good qualifications exist around the world, and registration, or membership, of one of the relevant societies provides a safety umbrella in the event of disputes. Sadly these are not uncommon or unlikely when you think of the complex needs of each individual horse and rider and the many influencing factors.

Each horse and rider combination is unique. To achieve the optimum performance from the saddle there must be a thorough understanding of the biomechanics of the horse at each stage of training, and the subtle changes that affect the balance and straightness of horse, rider and saddle. As the age and stage of training of the horse (and rider) progress, it's a good idea to keep a close eye on such changes and how they relate to the continuing good fit of the saddle. A saddle that appears to fit can cause problems if such issues are ignored, and the saddle can become a limiting factor if the fit or straightness is lost.

It is only when clear communication and understanding between all concerned is maintained that optimum performance is possible.

17 Farriery

Shoeing: 'Prevention is Better than the Cure.'

ROB RENIRIE

Rob is Dutch; he trained in Germany as a Bereiter (professional rider) and spent many years there as a rider/trainer. During those years he recognized just how difficult it was to find a good farrier, and so in 1975 he began training as a farrier. He qualified in 1977; in 1988 he also achieved a Master's degree in Therapeutic and Orthopaedic Shoeing.

Rob's riding career gives him a unique perspective; although quite a few farriers ride, not many have been through the Bereiter system, spent years as a rider/trainer, and – guessing now! – not too many have also gained a specialized university degree! He is world famous, both as the Dutch Olympic team farrier, and also as a result of his guest lectures, clinics and research. He is one of the most experienced farriers in the dressage world, and has many international and Olympic riders on his books. He presented a session at the 2009 Global Dressage Forum in Holland; we were very impressed by his straightforward and pragmatic approach to horses, dressage and shoeing, as was the rest of the audience of the world's top riders, trainers, judges and owners. He was invited back in 2010 by popular vote.

He has some basic precepts from which he tries never to deviate – dressage is about the exterior of the horse, the way that animal moves, and the right choices of material and

LEFT: *The farrier's craft.*

RIGHT: *Rob Renirie at the Global Dressage Forum in Holland, 2009. (Courtesy of Sjoert Pegge)*

shoes to keep the feet supported, protected, balanced and well shod. A good farrier can create a good-looking foot, but if the natural shape of the foot is changed, this can cause problems within the internal structures, such as the tendons. Horses need sufficient toe to absorb shock and to help create energy to take the next step; however, sufficient doesn't mean over-long, as this changes the dynamics of the foot to the detriment of the rest of its structures. The toes, together with the heels, bars and frogs, need to be able to work in conjunction with each other to cope with the stresses of movement.

It's very important to consider the shape of the leg and the external foot, but also particularly the pedal bone, to ensure that the angles are not altered. For this, Rob likes to see an x-ray of the foot, and also to see the horse moving in all paces: 'You can hear how a horse lands on his feet.' It is important not to change the natural function of the foot or the direction of the way in which the joints are by nature. If your farrier has never seen how your horse moves in walk and trot, how is he going to know the way in which the horse puts his feet to the ground, and thus how best he should be shod?

For preference, Rob would like to see as many horses as possible unshod. Think about wild horses: they cope without shoes, often on rough and uneven ground, and their hooves stay trimmed by nature. There's a school of opinion that worries about our modern sport horses that only ever work on surfaces and even ground – when they come across other 'normal' surfaces they don't cope too well. It could be that just shoeing them in front would be enough? Not all horses can go without shoes, but where a horse has strong feet, well looked after from a foal, this can go a long way towards problem-free feet and then the horse can be shod as simply as possible, with good materials and keeping close to the basics.

The coronary band usually makes the shape of the foot and thus the shoe. Rob doesn't use concave steel on dressage horses, preferring to use quite light flat steel (but not aluminium because it is very slippery) so that the shoe stays on top of the surface and allows the horse to turn easily. For front shoes, Rob prefers a slightly rolling toe that covers one third of the hoof wall. He thins the toe until it's wider by about 3mm, and then he lifts it a little bit, with no clips where possible, and small nails. He files as little as possible of the wall, wanting it to stay straight and strong. For hind shoes, he hammers the toe of the shoe to create a rounded toe so that it rolls easily; he doesn't take the toe too far back, and leaves only 4.5mm of the shoe over at the back.

Remedial shoeing to cope with cracks is best done by shoeing wider on the sides, thus taking the pressure off the crack. Some horses have one foot smaller than the other: this smaller foot always makes the leg higher, the bigger foot makes the leg lower. It's important to change the smaller foot rather than the larger one, in order to protect the structure of the leg and the joint, and this needs to be done gradually over a period of time.

Rob considers that it is more important that the horse is comfortable in the way the foot is trimmed, and with his shoes, than to create a beautiful look at all costs. Imagine how you would feel if someone came along and completely changed the structure of your feet in one go, and how such changes would affect your whole body; what nature gave you works quite well for you, and any changes should be gradual and minimal so that you can continue to function. (This is obviously a huge generalization, but we hope you get the point.) Think also about the undesirable long-term side effects of wearing fashion shoes and the possible crippling effects of doing so!

In our opinion there is no one better qualified than Rob to talk to you about shoeing, and his beliefs and priorities as a farrier.

Load-bearing at extreme levels of sport. Dressage exerts similar load-bearing extremes in most Grand Prix work.

I've been a farrier for thirty-four years, and am still finding out that many things have been invented and that many things have been tried out in connection with shoeing horses, and especially sport horses. After all these years, my observation is simply that traditional trimming or shoeing generally works the best. There is an English saying, 'Keep it simple, stupid!'. This is not to suggest that anyone is actually stupid, but that sometimes people think they need to over-complicate what is essentially very simple. *Protect rather than over-correct.* Farriery should follow the horse's natural shape, with as little interference as possible.

Naturally there have been many changes in equestrian use, but there have been more changes in how horses are kept, particularly for equestrian sports. For good sporting performance, competent care, guidance, training and implementation of these basic concepts are necessary. But in the case of extremes in high level equestrian sport, when potentially excessive demands are made of the horses, injuries occur more and more frequently, and solutions or stopgaps are sought to cope with these extremes.

Manufacturers are not slow in responding. The market is flooded with all sorts of soles, artificial horn, adhesives and other curiosities. Problems and errors made at a fundamental level of foot care can be treated with various stopgaps, and 'We'll see what we do about it next time' has become the philosophy, instead of addressing the problem head on in a more natural way. An example is the use of a shoe that is too fine for a normally thick hoof wall. Some people will then file away the wall, while others nail outside the white line; in both cases the wall deteriorates, leading to crumbling hooves, loose walls and so on. But is that a problem? No, of course not! There are plenty of synthetic resins or other adhesives for sale. Where is the limit for these stopgaps? It is fine that these materials are available to use in emergencies, but it was surely never intended that they should be used routinely for shoeing horses.

If stopgaps such as these are approached in the right way, they are a fantastic resource. But I must repeat that many problems arise from fundamental errors of shoeing. Besides this, should we not ask ourselves whether some horses are actually suitable for the intended discipline?

If a horse becomes injured, the advice in many cases is to trim the toes very short, and raise the heels (there are all sorts of wedge shapes). The pressure and differences in load are enormous; just think of the change in the flow and rhythm of movement. I always try to keep to the correct shoeing, and I do not deviate from this if there is a good shape, but necessity knows no law.

So long as everything goes smoothly, there are no problems, but when things go wrong, the basic concepts become important again. Toed-in or toed-out stance is not a major problem, but it can't be corrected in adult horses (although some corrections are possible for young animals). But if we need to make such changes to the stance of an adult horse, we should really ask again: is the horse suitable for the desired sport, or are certain professional groups or suppliers trying to line their pockets?

I want to give a warning against using remedies of every sort, whether appropriate or not, when the diagnosis is often poor, just to show the customer that something has been done. My personal experience is that many farriers are condemned for a relatively small number of horses that are taken to horse clinics, where faults are found with the

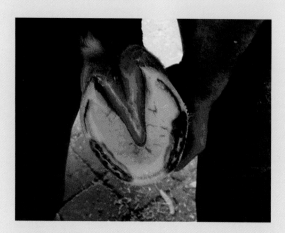

The frog laid bare; note its prominence within the foot structure.

shoeing, without anything being known about when the horse was last shod or what pressures the farrier was under to 'make the horse right'.

After all, farriery is a trade, no more and no less; co-operation between all interested parties is very important, without necessarily apportioning blame. It is this collaboration and consultation that ensures that a horse is shod well on the basis of a good diagnosis. These days we are also confronted with new disciplines, such as Western riding, where you need to deviate from the basic shoe forms to improve performance in the sport. The same applies to trotters and racehorses; this does not mean it encourages a longer life, but the sporting performance is seen as more important.

Harmonize training and quality, and take more time to learn about horses and their structures; don't just look for solutions when it is too late.

Now let's talk about whether I introduce minor or major corrections for adult sport horses. I try to provide horses whose natural conformation means they carry a heavy load on their front feet with a cushioning shoe, if that's necessary. However, many horses hate soles or inlay material as they often result in loss of feeling or reduced grip, which makes the horse lose confidence.

THE FROG

The frog is very important. It's a bit of a puzzle, partly on account of its funny shape and name, but more particularly because there is nothing like it in our own foot. It is necessary therefore to explain why nature has given the horse a frog and for what purpose. Actually the frog is quite one of the most interesting parts of the horse's whole body and shows nature in her most ingenious mood; in thinking of the frog you must regard it as a most effective natural anti-slipping and anti-concussion device.

You will appreciate that when a horse needs to pull up sharply or turn, there is a considerable risk of him slipping or straining himself unless he can obtain a secure grip on the ground. Likewise, when he gallops fast there must be considerable jar to the body at every step, leading eventually to lameness unless some means exists of deadening or absorbing the shock. The frog serves both purposes.

Let's see how it works. It acts as an anti-slipping device in the following ways. It is made of horn, but of a softer kind of horn than the wall or sole – indeed it is very much like a piece of India rubber, and just as rubber soles on a pair of shoes give you a grip on the ground, so it is with the horse's frog. This action is enhanced by the fact that, when a horse puts his foot to the ground, the frog region is the first part to make contact with the ground; in a fast turn he sticks his feet out, thereby compressing the frog even more.

When you jump over something in the gymnasium you are taught to land on your toes and not on your heels, because if you land on your heels, you suffer a very nasty jar to all the bones in your leg. By landing on your toes some of the shock of impact is dispersed before it reaches your leg bones.

The horse's frog acts in this way, and serves the purpose of preventing jar to the bones in the leg. This is very important, because constant jarring to the legs may well eventually lead to lameness.

Now let us see how the frog acts as a shock absorber. When the foot makes contact with the ground the frog yields slightly, so absorbing some of the jar. What jarring remains, is then transmitted upwards to a soft cushion which lies within the foot just above the frog. This, too, yields, but in an outward direction so forcing the heel apart. In other words, the impact is transmitted upwards and then dispersed outwards, thus saving a great deal of concussion from travelling up the bones of the leg.

The action of the frog also contributes greatly to the circulation of blood and oxygen in the foot and in the horse's legs. Since the circulatory process diminishes the further from the heart the structures lie, this is a necessary function of the frog for foot health.

GENERALITIES

Eggbar, heartbar and Belgian bar shoes, and the like, can be very useful in some cases to help these animals function better, but they should only be used when really necessary and should not become a fashion trend.

For horses that have a toed-in or toed-out stance, or high-angled or sharp-angled feet, it is necessary to try as much as possible to make the centre line through the foot straight, so the horse can land in as level a way as possible.

Make the time between shoeings shorter, as is customary in many countries, so that fewer differences in stance have time to develop: what is the point of a wedge or eggbar if it has completely disappeared into the heel after eight weeks? Shoe the horse with a well fitting shoe every five to six weeks (depending on the horn growth), and it will have fewer problems. The so-called 'full rock and roll' shoe is a good therapeutic aid, but is less suitable for use in top-level sport. (This is a full rolling-motion shoe that facilitates breakover laterally and medially, offering heel support, and constantly transferring load forces from painful to healthier areas of the foot.)

I find that most farriers and vets want to extend bar shoes too far back, behind the last extremity of the hoof capsule, thinking that this will support the horse's bodyweight. I have found that this is not always the case. In thinking about this problem over a period of time, I find that we tend to overlook the fact that the centre of balance is under the hoof capsule, as opposed to being under the centre of the extended shoe. Therefore, I personally do not shoe this far back behind the soft tissue. Eggbar and straight shoes will crush the heel area and hoof tubules severely. (Tubules are the constituent parts of the horny wall of the foot; they grow down from the coronet and are connected together by the sensitive laminae; damage to these tubules can cause abnormal growth and distortion of the foot shape.)

I have found that moving the bar shoe back under the hoof capsule is far more beneficial than using wedged bar shoes.

My personal finding is that if we raise the heel area of horses in training, they become tender in the soft tissue, shorten their stride, and put more stress on the extensor branches of the suspensory ligament. This tends to encourage them to land on the heel area. Instead, if we move the shoe back under the hoof, this seems to encourage them to extend their stride and land on the entire ground surface of the hoof. I roll, or at least breakover, the toe of most of the bar shoes I fit; in some cases I will use rocker-toe shoes.

One piece of advice I give my customers is to keep the horse in regular exercise, to maintain its general condition.

More and more often, there are situations involving people with little knowledge of horses, who don't have enough experience to accurately assess or 'read' the horse, and who think that only complicated (and expensive) procedures will be what's needed. I hope with all my heart that this exceptional animal, the horse, will be treated with respect and knowledge, and that absurdities in trade and sport will not gain the upper hand. We need to make sure that there are specialists who want to become farriers because of their love for horses and the job, and who have common sense and the courage to use it.

In this field, as in many other horse-related occupations, horse owners need to see the advantages of consulting the right professional.

Two of my main concerns are to emphasize the importance of calling in appropriate expertise, and that colleagues should not hesitate to consult each other in the case of problems and difficulties. This can help prevent a great deal of misery, primarily for the animal but also for the owner.

Remember the adage 'No foot, no horse', and also 'Keep it simple'. My colleagues and I cannot make a Fiat into a Ferrari, although many people think that this should be possible. A tuned-up Fiat is in the garage for repairs more often than a Ferrari – but this does depend upon the Ferrari being driven correctly!

18 Rider Posture and Biomechanics

The habitual standing posture of the rider whilst off the horse will largely determine the efficiency and effectiveness of his or her riding position.

Certainly there are many riders whose skill remains high despite poor posture, but in company with most sports, the more efficient the posture, the more effective the sports person can be.

So what constitutes an efficient or 'correct' posture? Essentially, optimal postural alignment allows for the body parts to be arranged in such a way that they are in a state of balance, enabling the supporting body structures – bones, joints, ligaments, tendons, muscles and fascia (a thin sheath of fibrous tissue enclosing a muscle or other organ) – to do their job without injury and/or progressive deformity or degeneration.

Therefore, good posture facilitates minimal muscular effort and minimal joint loading, reducing the total energy and effort required for a given physical task while minimizing the physical stresses applied to the body.

The earth's gravitational field exerts a continuous and inescapable force. It makes sense, then, for a body to adopt an easy upright alignment where the effects of gravity are distributed in such a way that no one structure or area is overstressed – here you could take 'body' to mean either a physical being or an inanimate object such as a building. However, the position of the line of gravity through the skeleton determines both the degree of

ABOVE: *Before: With Liz Launder (right) and Hercules (the horse). Computer-generated coloured lines clearly indicate angles and lines. (© 1997–2009 Quintic Consultancy Ltd. All rights reserved)*

BELOW: *After: A big difference to the rider's position, but breathing would be good! (© 2004–2009 Equinalysis Ltd. All rights reserved)*

muscular effort involved in maintaining all phases of posture, and the body's success in resisting displacement – in other words, how well balanced a person is. Riders are unique in that they need to be able both to resist the forces of displacement produced by the horse's movement, whilst simultaneously being able to influence that movement.

Shifts in body alignment will change the line of gravity and reduce the balance of the rider, compromising the control of the horse and/or requiring effort to stay in balance, thus reducing the rider's effectiveness. This is seen in the extreme with a novice rider who is displaced all over the place by the horse's movement, but it applies also to the most skilful rider who may be using strength to remain in position, rather than the effortless balance that comes from optimal posture.

Optimal posture, although positional and dependent on the juxtaposition of the body parts, is, therefore, also dependent on the relative muscle balance between agonist, antagonist, and synergistic groups, or front, back, side to side, and left and right rotators. As an example, think of someone with a 'head forward' position (quite common in dressage riders). Gravity will be directed down through the head, so the muscles at the back of the neck at the top will have to contract or shorten and tense to oppose the weight of the head pulling to the ground. An immediate imbalance between the muscle balance of the front and back of the body is created, requiring effort to be given to maintaining an upright posture, and reducing effort-free balance.

So does rider position/posture have any impact on the performance of the horse other than that of control? Both a sport and a leisure pursuit, horse riding is huge worldwide and has, therefore, become of interest to scientists.

Research carried out to date has concluded that asymmetric loads applied to a horse's back negatively influence the normal kinematics or movement of the spine – a case for a symmetrical, well balanced rider. Whilst weight and the saddle have been shown (unsurprisingly) to cause overall extension (hollowing) of the horse's back and increased backward movement of the forelimb, minimizing the load applied and its displacement (a balanced or correct posture) is again supported.

Sitting trot has been also been seen to change the load applied to the hoof wall medially, while a forward seat directs the load laterally, with rising trot allowing a more uniform load to the hoof wall. [Authors' note: this is not, of itself, a reason for all dressage riders to opt for a rising trot.]

These are just a few examples of scientific knowledge which support the potential for negative influence, by the rider, on the horse's movement and carriage. Simultaneously they give value to the premise that good posture on and off the ground is an absolute requirement for the horseman.

● We are indebted to Liz Launder for her contribution to this subject. *See* Further Information on page 172.

WHAT IS BIOMECHANICS AND HOW DOES IT RELATE TO DRESSAGE?

Sports biomechanics is a diverse inter-disciplinary science, incorporating bio-engineering, human and equine performance, zoology, orthopaedics, physical anthropology, anatomy, physiology and botany! It applies the laws of mechanics and physics to human and equine performance in order to understand what roles the physical principles of motion, resistance, momentum and friction play in sport, and in our case, dressage.

Simulation, measurement and analysis of the external and internal forces that come to bear when horses and riders perform various movements are the basis of understanding the mechanical cause and effect aspects involved. In other words, it's the science behind understanding how we and our horses use our body structures (anatomy) to achieve motion and performance (function).

What do Biomechanics, Movement Analysis and Gait Analysis Mean?

The study of biomechanics is essentially the study of movement and everything that affects it. Biomechanics is used in most other sports, including athletics, tennis, swimming and skiing. Within the dressage world, biomechanics has several useful applications which can support the owner, rider and trainer in helping to improve and maintain the horse's performance.

How Does it Work?

Biomechanics was first investigated by Edward Muybridge (1830–1904). This interesting character is worth looking up on the internet to read his fascinating personal history. He was the first to use film and photographs to show that the trot has a moment of suspension. He used a series of cameras set on a trigger mechanism to capture the limb sequence – a stark comparison to the techniques available today.

From these initial findings, interest has grown to the point where this field is rapidly becoming one of the largest branches of equine sport science.

These days, much sophisticated equipment is available, such as three-dimensional (3D) and 2D motion analysis systems, 2D video analysis systems, force plates and pressure systems. Another system is Quintic Biomechanics, which uses the application of markers to the horse to identify joint centres/rotations to the computer system. This information is technically processed to display quantified information in a 2D view, which relates solely to the horse's movement.

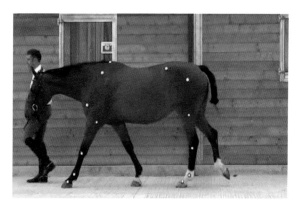

ABOVE: *White markers for tracking joint centres, picked up by the digital camera.*

BELOW: *Digitized – multi-trace lines and colours all have meanings, perhaps velocity or angle changes, which are then analysed to obtain patterns of the horse's movement. (Courtesy of Centaur Biomechanics)*

In the first picture, markers have been applied to the horse, the locations of which have been revealed by manual palpation of anatomical landmarks such as the elbow, carpal, fetlock, pastern, which identify joint centres and rotations. The markers are then joined together through a process called 'tracking': in this way, quantified data is produced and it is possible to tell, for example, if one limb is flexing more than the other, and if so, by how much. Without the markers it is not possible to identify the joint centres, and the data would be unreliable and unquantifiable.

The second picture on page 165 demonstrates the process known as 'multi-trace', which is the next stage of an assessment that has been 'digitized'. In this process all files go through the computer, from whence statistical data is extracted that relates solely to the horse's movement. Each marker connects to the other and creates a link between the top and bottom markers. Each line and colour has a meaning – either there is a change in angle between three markers, or in the velocity or the acceleration with which a marker travels from start to finish – and all this information is stored in the system. An operator would extract the required statistics and export them to a statistical package where comparisons are made from left to right to establish the patterns of movement.

The picture below left illustrates the graphs that are the final stage of the multi-trace process, where all files have been digitized and analysed through the software's statistical analysis suite. The data is then used to create various comparisons, such as the difference between left and right carpal flexion, or left and right fetlock hyperextension, or the differences between left and right tarsal flexion. The first graph illustrates carpal flexion, and it is clear that the left and right limbs follow a similar pattern, which is as it should be. In the second graph there is a clear difference between left and right, which indicates carpal asymmetry, as the right carpal joint is more flexed than the left.

This is only one of the measurements that can be used to demonstrate the output of the system. Carpal and tarsal flexion, fetlock hyperextension, forelimb and hindlimb protraction and retraction, stance duration, stride time, and velocity, are all assessed, together with other criteria, to produce a detailed account of a particular horse's movement.

Nearly all joints can be assessed. However, due to skin displacement, some joints are less easy to assess. For example, the stifle is notoriously difficult to assess owing to the large amount of skin movement in that area; therefore a second protocol is generally employed in order to explore this region further.

Graph 1

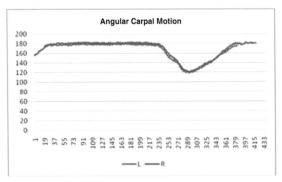

Graph 2

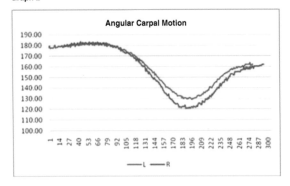

The pictures are transformed into graphs, from which the final assessments of the movement patterns are made. (Courtesy of Centaur Biomechanics)

Biomechanical Assessment for Physiotherapists

Biomechanics is used to good effect by physiotherapists as a way of ascertaining a horse's baseline (natural) movement, and identifying any movement restraints that could be improved or alleviated with physiotherapeutic intervention in the form of specific exercises.

The key benefit of biomechanical assessment is the ability to store and repeat the data collection, and in this way, two sets of data can be provided, the 'before' and 'after', to see and evaluate what benefits and changes have been achieved by the physiotherapist's intervention. If there is improvement in the range of movement and/or joint mobility, obviously this would suggest that the treatment plan has been successful.

Biomechanical Investigation into Saddle Pressure

Research into the effect that different saddles have on horses' movement has been carried out for a few years now. The questions addressed are: does one saddle help improve the horse's movement when compared with another? And, if so, by how much? The results from such investigations have been interesting, with some saddles helping to reduce hind limb asymmetry and aid hind limb power production.

In addition to motion analysis, there is also the Novel Pliance system, operated by the Society of Master Saddlers and the BEF. The Pliance system is a pressure-mapping mat that sits underneath the saddle. Data relating to the pressure exerted on the horse's back is transmitted, via a data logger, to a laptop which instantly displays the given pressure underneath the saddle and the rider's centre of mass (COM) at any one time. This information is then married up with the motion analysis data to see, firstly, if particular saddles exert less pressure, and secondly, to see if they help improve movement. In most cases there has been a positive relationship between less pressure and increased movement.

Biomechanical Analysis for the Rider

Riders should view themselves as athletes. As with athletes in other sports, biomechanics forms a large part of the training programme, as it has been proven to be a valid tool in facilitating performance.

The way in which a rider sits on a horse greatly influences that horse. For example, a rider who sits crookedly affects the horse's way of going, and how it develops through its training. Sessions combining osteopathic assessment with video analysis at the UK's Hartpury College Equine Therapy and Rehabilitation Centre form part of the Rider Performance Analysis Clinics and incorporate the use of a mechanical horse. The benefits of a mechanical horse are that the environment is controlled, so that the variables of a horse's influence are removed, and analysis can focus solely on the rider.

As with the horse's movement, the rider is marked with white dots so that the computer can pick up the physical characteristics of his posture and movement. In this way, physiotherapeutic assessment and intervention can be monitored 'before' and 'after', to show the rider what improvements could, and should, be made, and a physiotherapeutic report is drawn up, with recommended exercises for each rider.

In addition, a dressage analysis has been devised, where the rider's position is assessed during a test, as a way of optimizing his marks, as it has become evident that the way the rider sits correlates to the way the horse performs.

This type of assessment has proved very useful to both riders and trainers, as any weakness or postural asymmetries are easy to see and assess. It is important to note that such an assessment is, in essence, a step on the road to improvement (and it often reflects what the trainer sees and tries to correct!). The journey requires continued input and collaboration from the trainer, the rider and the physiotherapist, with regular monitoring to ensure that the rider is progressing as planned.

Assessments are also carried out off the horse, with markers being placed on the rider, who then performs a series of exercises. From the trials that have been carried out, it is clear that there is a strong correlation between the asymmetries observed when the rider is dismounted, and those seen when he is mounted. This indicates something underlined many times throughout this book, that our everyday posture is mirrored in positional weaknesses when we are riding.

Biomechanical Analysis and the Farrier

Over the years the saying 'No foot, no horse' has been familiar throughout the industry from grass roots to professional, and is very true. Basically, the way the foot is balanced and managed has a direct effect on the horse's movement and performance.

Domestic and team farriers have looked at foot balance via the ability of the video analysis systems and cameras to capture movement at 300 frames per second, and this work has proved most valuable. To put this into context, the human eye can only manage approximately twelve frames per second. Such high speed analysis therefore allows for information that is approximately twenty-five times more detailed to be obtained about the feet and how they are put to the ground, which directly affects the way in which the feet should be balanced and shod.

As before, pre- and post assessments are common to evaluate any changes and improvements.

Biomechanical Analysis and Veterinary Associates

Biomechanics is increasingly valued by veterinarians as part of the initial and ongoing clinical assessment of a horse. It has been used in cases where a horse is 'not quite right', and biomechanical analysis has highlighted asymmetric areas, which have then been investigated and subsequently treated.

Biomechanics is also used post treatment to assist in the evaluation of how much a horse has progressed.

Biomechanical Assessment and Owners

From 2006 up until 2010 over 700 horses have been analysed, of which 60 per cent have been screening assessments requested by the owners. The main reason for such requests is usually because they wish to see exactly how their horses move, and in dressage this element is scrutinized in every training session.

Not only does an assessment look at the way in which the horse moves, it also looks at any weakness that could be identified and supported, thus helping to prevent injury and maximize performance. By early investigation before any problems manifest themselves, such analysis allows rapid support and treatment to be instigated, which helps to keep the horses 'on the road' for longer, from either a performance and/or a health aspect.

The benefits of similar analyses are available to all riders and horses.

- We are indebted to Russell Guire at Centaur Biomechanics for his contribution to this subject (*see* Further Information on page 172).

Conclusion

*One who believes that he has mastered the art of horsemanship
has not yet begun to understand the horse.*

(Unknown)

It is difficult to translate or interpret theory, words, feel and experience into action. The most essential messages that horses and riders need to appreciate is that the horse must go forwards and be in balance. The Scales of Training are too often used in a training situation without their meaning being truly appreciated. Until you have your horse stretching forwards to the bit, relaxed and loose over the back, working from behind, and going forwards in a balanced way, you will struggle to have rhythm, or suppleness, or contact, or straightness, or impulsion – or collection.

Emotionally, dressage riders need considerable self-discipline to remain calm and focused enough to respond appropriately in all circumstances. Then you can evaluate your horse's responses and be ready with praise and appreciation or, on the occasions when you think that he is wilfully misunderstanding or being 'naughty', you can deal with it and move on.

You must be able to do again what you did yesterday, and to understand that you might be doing something very similar again tomorrow – or not. You should be totally flexible and open-minded so that your training is tuned to each horse, individually, whilst keeping the Scales of Training firmly in mind. The balance so essential to horse and rider in a physical way is also just as crucial to both from a mental standpoint.

Horses learn by repetition. Leaving gaps in the horse's basic training will undoubtedly result in shortcomings at a later stage, a lack of ability and confidence that will prevent your being able to progress when you want to move on to more difficult work at the higher levels.

Willingness is an innate quality, and one that should be nurtured both on the ground and when riding so that your horse is 'on your side', relaxed and happy to have attention. Even the

Natural talent.

most willing horse's attitude can be destroyed by inconsistency, incorrect handling or unreasonable requests. Riders need to find a way to have their horses work for them and analyse why things go wrong, or are wrong, and in general should blame themselves. Horses respond to stress with stress; they respond to relaxation with relaxation.

Be aware that not all horses are suited to a career in dressage, perhaps by temperament or maybe conformation, and sometimes the best policy is to recognize their shortcomings and find something they do enjoy – jumping, hunting, hacking out – and incorporate these activities into their work, or perhaps change their career. Furthermore, too much specialization too early can overburden a young horse, and may set him on a course that might not be the best one for him.

- Sometimes accepting your own limitations, and those of your horse, can be very liberating for all concerned. This is not to say, however, that you should give up the moment things become difficult or challenging.

To achieve lasting satisfaction and success, one has to rely on a combination of tenacity, emotional strength, dedication, knowledge, talent, hard work and good training – and also luck: 'The more I practise, the luckier I get!' When you find the 'right' horse with whom to share that satisfaction and success, always supposing that he stays sound long enough for that to happen, you can consider yourself 'lucky'.

In many ways the 'character' of your horse, how he behaves, and his way of going are

Natural balance and activity.

quite probably a direct reflection of who you are and how you live your life. Close attention to the horse's welfare pays dividends. Preventative care from the 'team' might seem unnecessary – 'If it ain't broke, don't fix it!' – but regular check-ups can often reveal the early stages of potentially expensive and damaging problems. By the time whatever is wrong finally manifests itself, it is often a long journey back to fitness.

It is also true that there is no such thing as a 'perfect' horse, sound and without any physical problems during his working life, so sometimes you have to deal with it and then just get on and ride! If they could, horses would doubtless argue that there's no such thing as a perfect human!

We are personally convinced that the modern penchant for instant gratification doesn't 'fit' with a life with horses. It takes the time it takes to find and fit the various pieces of the training jigsaw, and there's never a point at which you know everything or have learned everything. One way and another, horses have a way of bringing us all down to earth (sometimes literally!).

In this book you have a truly German/English approach – she's German, I'm English. It has been interesting to consider the different cultural approaches; we've worked together for many years and have always enjoyed what the media describe as 'a full and frank exchange of ideas' (but in a good way!) – however, one thing on which we did agree is that we'd try to make this book accessible from a language perspective whilst keeping the German approach to training intact, albeit with an Anglo-Saxon slant! We hope we have managed to do this.

The contents of this book are a mixture of our thoughts, ideas, experience and experiences, plus knowledge gleaned from other riders and trainers; from books, articles, reviews, seminars, clinics and forums put forward by much more knowledgeable people than us, condensed, if

Angela Niemeyer Eastwood with Hemingway.

that's the right word, or perhaps distilled, into the best effort we could make.

Horses have given us a wonderful life; we have been places, met people, and had opportunities that probably only the world of horses could have provided. We've also had great heartache, disappointment, disillusion and sadness – but life provides these things anyway.

We hope you find this book readable and useful, and we wish you the best of good luck and happiness with your horses.

Here is nobility without conceit,
friendship without envy,
beauty without vanity.
A willing servant yet never a slave.

(Ronald Duncan)

Further Information

Beavis, Jo
Founded in 1992, the National Saddle Centre offers a wide selection of saddles for all disciplines.
www.nationalsaddlecentre.co.uk

Boldt, Harry
Das Dressurpferd (otherwise known as 'The Big Black Book'), published in Germany in 1997. The photography is amazing and worthy of lengthy study; the text is in German but don't let that put you off. It cost about £50 in 1997; now (2010), available on Amazon, prices vary from €350 to $800!

Fitflops
Like ordinary flipflops, with a thick sole, easy and supportive to walk in; they help with balance, coordination and joint relief, and improve muscle tone. Their cost is similar to trainers and 'normal' shoes; they are quite stylish, and there are some closed Fitflops so that socks can be worn.
www.fitflops.com

Guire, Russell
25 Oaktree Close, Moreton Morell, Warks, CV35 9BB Tel: 07788 978627
info@centaurbiomechanics.co.uk
www.centaurbiomechanics.co.uk

Hall, Joanna
Joanna Hall is one of the UK's leading fitness, diet and lifestyle experts; walking is the foundation of what she does, and she and her team are passionate about its benefits.
www.joannahall.com

Launder, Liz
BSc. Hons (Biol. Sci.), BSc. Hons (Ost.), MSc. Poor performance and sports injury specialist – human and equine.
Hardwick Hay Farm, Link End Road, Corse Lawn, Glos GL19 4NN Tel: 07950 119724
www.osteopathy4horses.co.uk

MTB (Masai Barefoot Technology)
MTB shoes replicate barefoot walking: they work the leg and buttock muscles, relieve back and joint pain, and improve balance. They are tricky to walk in, but it is worth persevering with them. They are not very stylish, and are relatively expensive. Stockists online (type in 'Masai Barefoot Technology') and in the shops.

Meyners, Dr Eckart/BALIMO Stool
BALance In MOtion. This stool enables mobilization and expansion of the mobility of the pelvic area, reactivating the spine function through soft but complex movements, training the muscles in the back, neck and head, and positively influencing the symmetry of the lower back and abdominal muscles, through balancing exercises off the horse.
It is particularly designed to require the sitter to find a balance so that the stool becomes stable – the top is capable of total rotation. The circular movement mobilizes the whole of the

pelvis, and done properly, makes an extraordinary difference within a few days. Developed by Dr Eckart Meyners, Professor of Movement Theory, Health Theory, and Equestrian Education Science at Lueneburg University, in Germany.
www.balimo.de

Micklem Competition Bridle
www.williammicklem.com

Rider Performance Clinics
At the time of writing, Hartpury College (UK) runs a scientifically based clinic using IT biomechanical technology (Russell Guire), the experience and expertise of the osteopath (Liz Launder) who specializes in horses and humans, and Hercules, the long-suffering horse simulator. A blueprint of the rider's posture, advice, exercises and a DVD enables each person to maximize the correct use of his/her body on the horse.
www.hartpury.ac.uk

Rebounder
Mini-exercise 'trampoline' but less bouncy and more firmly strung; comes with a support handle to help with balance. The rebounder works because your body is constantly re-balancing itself just to stay upright. A big range of exercises is possible. It is moderately expensive. Herewith an extract from their website: 'Beginning with as little as 30 seconds a day you can: Increase your vitality; Burn excess fat; Improve muscle tone; Lower cholesterol level; Improve circulation; Improve balance and co-ordination.'
www.supertrampdirect.co.uk

We hope that you'll find some of the above useful, and a start for further information.

Bibliography

Bell, J. (Compiler) *101 Exercises from Top Riders* (David Charles, 2007).

Buerger, U. and Zietzschmann, O. *Der Reiter Formt das Pferd* (FN Verlag, 1987).

Busch, C. L. *Die Hilfengebung des Reiters* (Cadmos Verlag, 2000).

Clarke, S. *Dressage Dreams 10* (Lewis Harding, 2009).

Collins, D. (Compiler) *Dressage Masters* (The Lyons Press, 2006).

von Dietze, S. *Balance in Movement* (J. A. Allen and Co., 1999).

FEI Working Committee, *FEI Dressage Handbook; Guidelines for Judging* (Fédération Équestre International, 2007).

German National Federation *The Principles of Riding* (Kenilworth Press, 2000).

German National Federation *Die Deutsche Reitlehre* (FN Verlag, 2000).

Heuschmann, Dr G. *Tug of War: Classical versus 'Modern' Dressage* (Trafalgar Square Books, 2007).

Higgins, G. *How Your Horse Moves* (David and Charles, 2009).

Hinnemann, J. and van Baalen, C. *The Simplicity of Dressage* (J. A. Allen, 2003).

Karl, P. *Twisted Truths of Modern Dressage* (Cadmos Verlag, 2008).

Klimke, Dr R., *Grundausbildung des Jungen Reitpferdes* (Franckh'sche Verlagshandlung, 1984).

Kyrklund, K. and Lemkow, J. *Dressage with Kyra* (Kenilworth Press, 1998).

Meyners, Dr E. *Das Bewegungsgefuehl des Reiters* (Franckh-Kosmos Verlag, 2003).

Meyners, Dr E. *Aufwaerm-programm fuer Reiter* (Franckh-Kosmos, 2008).

Niggli, W. M. *Dressage – a Guideline for Riders and Judges* (J. A. Allen, 2003).

Prockl, E. *Wenn Erwachsene in den Sattel Wollen* (Cadmos Verlag, 1998).

Rachen-Schoeneich, G. and Schoeneich, K. *Correct Movement in Horses; Improving Straightness and Balance* (Kenilworth Press, 2007).

Steiner, B. *Mind, Body and Spirit* (Kenilworth Press, 2003).

Stubbs, Dr N.C. and Clayton, Dr H. M. *Activate Your Horse's Core* (Sports Horse Publications, 2008)

Zettl, W. *Dressage in Harmony* (Half Halt Press Inc., 1998)

JOURNALS

British Dressage Magazine, Greenshires Publishing

BD Rules, British Dressage

Dressage Today (USA) Source Interlink Magazines

Global Forum (Holland) reports, Andrea Hessay

Reiter Revue (Germany), Paul Parey Zeitschriftenverlag

Index